FORERUNNERS: IDEAS FIRST FROM THE UNIVERSITY OF
MINNESOTA PRESS

Original e-works to spark new scholarship

FORERUNNERS: IDEAS FIRST is a thought-in-process series of break-
through digital works. Written between fresh ideas and finished books,
Forerunners draws on scholarly work initiated in notable blogs, social
media, conference plenaries, journal articles, and the synergy of academic exchange. This is gray literature publishing: where intense
thinking, change, and speculation take place in scholarship.

Clare Birchall
**Shareveillance: The Dangers of Openly Sharing and
Covertly Collecting Data**

Ian Bogost
The Geek's Chihuahua: Living with A

William E. Connolly
**Aspirational Fascism: The Struggle fc
under Trumpism**

T0168703

Andrew Culp
Dark Deleuze

Sohail Daulatzai
Fifty Years of "The Battle of Algiers": Past as Prologue

Grant Farred
Martin Heidegger Saved My Life

David Golumbia
The Politics of Bitcoin: Software as Right-Wing Extremism

Gary Hall
The Uberfication of the University

John Hartigan Jr.
Aesop's Anthropology: A Multispecies Approach

Mark Jarzombek
Digital Stockholm Syndrome in the Post-Ontological Age

Nicholas A. Knouf
How Noise Matters to Finance

A Billion Black Anthropocenes or None

A Billion Black Anthropocenes or None

Kathryn Yusoff

University of Minnesota Press

MINNEAPOLIS

The University of Minnesota Press
111 Third Avenue South, Suite 290
Minneapolis, MN 55401-2520
http://www.upress.umn.edu

Printed in the United States of America on acid-free paper

The University of Minnesota is an equal-opportunity educator and employer.

Versa 2021

The problem was gravity and the answer was gravity

—DIONNE BRAND, *Love Enough*

Thought of the Other is the moral generosity disposing me to accept the principle of alterity, to conceive of the world as not simple and straightforward, with only one truth—mine. But thought of the Other can dwell within me, without making me alter course, without "prizing me open," without changing me within myself. An ethical principle, it is enough that I not violate it.

The other of Thought is precisely this altering. Then I have to act . . . I change, and I exchange. This is an aesthetics of turbulence whose corresponding ethics is not provided in advance.

—ÉDOUARD GLISSANT, *Poetics of Relation*

Contents

Preface

This work started as a redress to the White Geology of the Anthropocene and found the guts of its mattering in the critical black feminist work of Sadiya Hartman's *Scenes of Subjection* and the alluvial subjectivity of the Martinique poets Aimé Césaire and Édouard Glissant. Hanging out in the interdisciplinary spaces opened and sustained by these works, many other feminist black scholars have been crucial to the approaches developed in this book. While unable to give this work its full due here, I am particularly grateful for the courageous analytical and politically poetic work of N. K. Jemisin's bringing together of race and geology across the rifts of broken earths, Sylvia Wynter's metamorphosis of a black biopolitics, Tina Campt's quiet futurity of images, Hortense Spillers's grammars of dissent, Katherine McKittrick's commitment to liberatory black geographies, Denise Ferreira da Silva's location of the foundational inscriptions of race in global geography, Tiffany King's ecologies, Michelle Wright's challenge to linear time-space, Elizabeth Povinelli's indigenous analytics that refuse redemption, Angela Last's critical Caribbean geopolitics, Christina Sharpe's atmospheres, and Fred Moten's writing in the blur. Through the completion of this work, it was Dionne Brand's writing that kept me company at 2:00 A.M. Her poetic relation, given without the possibility of resettling, insists that you must stay with and in the displacement. In that poetics, in its most material geographies, I found the new languages and structures of thought that a turn of epoch, the end of the world of Empire, seems to require. If there is what Brand (2001) calls a *Ruttier*—an oral poem that functioned as a map for sailors—recited throughout this text, its diasporic yearnings are listing toward the possibility of a gravity that defies antiblackness (in all its guises, across the black and brown commons forged in the afterlives of invasion, genocide, slavery, and settler colonialism). It is from Brand that I take an understanding of Blackness as a material vector that opens out new geographies of space and time that make fierce departures from the subjugating cuts in geography exorcised by imperial conditions. Blackness is understood as a state of relation (in Glissant's sense of the word) that is assigned to difference through a material colonial inscription, which simultaneously enacted the cutting of geographical ties to land and attachments to ecologies. These diasporic subjects that are summoned here are the ghosts of geology's epistemic and material modes of categorization and dispossession, which sit "beside the earth's own coiled velocities, its meteoric elegance" (Brand 2006, 100).

Another way to conceive this would be to understand Blackness as a historically constituted and intentionally enacted deformation in the formation of subjectivity, a deformation that presses an inhuman categorization and the inhuman earth into intimacy. This contact point of geographical proximity with the earth was constructed specifically as a node of extraction of properties and personhood. At the same time, this forced intimacy with the inhuman was repurposed for survival and formed into a praxis for remaking other selves that were built in the harshest of conditions. The proximity of black and brown bodies to harm in this intimacy with the inhuman is what I am calling *Black Anthropocenes*. It is an inhuman proximity organized by historical geographies of extraction, grammars of geology, imperial global geographies, and contemporary environmental racism. It is predicated on the presumed absorbent qualities of black and brown bodies to take up the body burdens of exposure to toxicities and to buffer the violence of the earth. Literally stretching black and brown bodies across the seismic fault lines of the earth, Black Anthropocenes subtend White Geology as a material stratum.

While genocide (and ongoing settler colonialism) and slavery (and its afterlives) are by no means historically or culturally assimilate, as they have different critical discourses, not to mention territorial implications, that are put into contact through the legacy of White Geology and its geographical and subjective dispossession. This White Geology continues to propagate imaginaries that organize Blackness as a stratum or seismic barrier to the costs of extraction, across the coal face, the alluvial planes, and the sugarcane fields, and on the slave block, into the black communities that buffer the petrochemical industries and hurricanes to the indigenous reservations that soak up the waste of industrialization and the sociosexual effects of extraction cultures. If the Anthropocene proclaims a sudden concern with the exposures of environmental harm to white liberal communities, it does so in the wake of histories in which these harms have been knowingly exported to black and brown communities under the rubric of civilization, progress, modernization, and capitalism. The Anthropocene might seem to offer a dystopic future that laments the end of the world, but imperialism and ongoing (settler) colonialisms have been ending worlds for as long as they have been in existence. The Anthropocene as a politically infused geology and scientific/popular discourse is just now noticing the extinction it has chosen to continually overlook in the making of its modernity and freedom.

In the context of this selective perspectivism, *Black Anthropocenes* marks an interjection or erasure that is a billion missing articulations of geologic events to provide a counterforce or gravity to the historical junctures from 1492 to 1950 (under consideration by the Anthropocene Working Group for the initiation event of the epoch). I want to challenge the racial blindness of the Anthropocene as a willful blindness that permeates its comfortable suppositions and its imaginaries of the planetary—imaginaries that constitute its geographies of concern and attribution. As an erasure that is both performed and obscured in the "point and erase" action of the naming of the Golden Spikes, Blackness is a material index of resistance to the projection of this Anthropocenic New World–Old World globalizing geography. Refusing the neat placing of Anthropocene geosocial "events" in geology and the reverberations of colonization that they represent, I offer an altered thinking in concert with a billion Black Anthropocenes as a change of register. A billion Black Anthropocenes names the all too many *voidings* of experiences that span multiple scales, manifestations, and ongoing extractive economies, in terms of the materiality and grammars that inculcate antiblackness through a material geophysics of race. In this book, the writers of the Caribbean are read as both counteraesthetic and counteranalytic to the carceral geo-logics of white settlers in colonialism and New World slavery. While the book sketches a limited engagement with the diverse histories of black and indigenous studies, it instead tries to stay with these geographies of the Caribbean and Americas as inchoate *within* the settler states of North America and Europe. In the spirit of Brand's poetics of maroonage and Wynter's concept of replantation, I have prioritized a patternation of thought and practice in the inscription of geology rather than a more exacting genealogy.[1] In the apprehension of geologic acts that underpin the Anthropocene-in-the-making, I recognize geology as a racial formation from the onset and, in its praxis, as an extractive and theoretical discipline.

1. This work is forthcoming in the book *Geologic Life*.

Geology, Race, and Matter

Let's start with the end of the world, why don't we?
—N. K. JEMISIN, *The Fifth Season*

Every generation confronts the task of choosing its past.
Inheritances are chosen as much as they are passed on. The
past depends less on "what happened then" than on the
desires and discontents of the present. Strivings and failures
shape the stories we tell. What we recall has as much to do
with the terrible things we hope to avoid as with the good
life for which we yearn. But when does one decide to stop
looking to the past and instead conceive of a new order?
When is it time to dream of another country or to embrace
other strangers as allies or to make an opening, an overture,
where there is none? When is it clear that the old life is over,
a new one has begun, and there is no looking back? From
the holding cell was it possible to see beyond the end of the
world and to imagine living and breathing again?

—SAIDIYA HARTMAN, *Lose Your Mother: A Journey along the
Atlantic Slave Route*

Across the spaces and places of geology, its languages of description and dispossession, the question of the Anthropocene shapeshifts, world making in epochal pronouncements of the "New World" of humanity, world breaking in the formation of the "Ends" of master subjects: Man, History, Civilization. In its brief tenure, the Anthropocene has metamorphosed. It has been taken up in the world, purposed, and put to work as a conceptual grab,

1

materialist history, and cautionary tale of planetary predicament. Equally, this planetary analytic has failed to do the work to properly identify its *own* histories of colonial earth-writing, to name the masters of broken earths, and to redress the legacy of racialized subjects that geology leaves in its wake. It has failed to grabble with the inheritance of violent dispossession of indigenous land under the auspices of a colonial geo-logics or to address the extractive grammars of geology that labor in the instrumentation and instrumentalization of dominant colonial narratives and their subjective, often subjugating registers that are an ongoing praxis of displacement.

Modern liberalism is forged through colonial violence, and slavery is at least coterminus with its ideas and experiences of freedom, if not with the material root of its historical possibility. Thus the ways in which geology underwrites that continuum—of liberal subjectivity and its historicity—and how geology as a praxis materially carries this relation into the future should matter in an epochal swerve. As the Anthropocene proclaims the language of species life—*anthropos*—through a universalist geologic commons, it neatly erases histories of racism that were incubated through the regulatory structure of geologic relations. The racial categorization of Blackness shares its natality with mining the New World, as does the material impetus for colonialism in the first instance. This means that the idea of Blackness and the displacement and eradication of indigenous peoples get caught and defined in the ontological wake of geology. The human and its subcategory, the inhuman, are historically relational to a discourse of settler-colonial rights and the material practices of extraction, which is to say that the categorization of matter is a spatial execution, of place, land, and person cut from relation through geographic displacement (and relocation through forced settlement and transatlantic slavery). That is, racialization belongs to a material categorization of the division of matter (corporeal and mineralogical) into active and inert. Extractable matter must be both passive (awaiting extraction and possessing of properties) and able to be activated through the mastery of white men. Historically, both slaves and gold have to be material and epistemically made through the recognition and extraction of their inhuman properties. These historic geologic relations and geo-logics span Europe, the Americas, Africa, and Asia through the movement of people, objects, and racial and material categories. Thus becoming postracial through Anthropocenic speciation is a foil of the humanist trickster (Yusoff and Thomas 2018)—one that places an injunction on the recognition of historic modes of geopolitical mattering while maintaining unequal relations of power through continued environmental exposures.

In this moment of reinscribing geology as a property of personhood in the Anthropocene (in the strategy of geologizing the social and socializing the geologic), there is a need to think with its former lives of inscription, not just those currently searched for in the strata. Or, to put it another way, what modes of *geologic life*[1] (material and psychic) are already imbricated in geologic practices, often in violent ways? Geology is a mode of accumulation, on one hand, and of dispossession, on the other, depending on which side of the geologic color line you end up on. In this book, I ask how geology is being reelaborated in the Anthropocene and consider what historicity would resist framing this epoch as a "new" condition that forgets its histories of oppression and dispossession. This project seeks to write a prehistory that is sufficient to the radical ambivalence of the *afterlives of geology*—of indigenous dispossession of land and sovereignty in the invasion of the Americas through to the ongoing petropolitics of settler colonialism; of slavery, "breaking rocks on the chain gang" (as Nina Simone sings it), to the current incarnations of antiblackness in mining black gold; and of the racialized impacts of climate change.

---

1. When I use the term *geologic life*, I do so to signal the corporeality of geology as a material embodiment and a systematic framing of materiality that has geopolitical and biopolitical consequences for the possibilities of being and nonbeing (see Yusoff 2013, 2015, 2018).

To redress *how* geology makes property relations and properties a relation of subjugation is to challenge the incompleteness of address in the Anthropocene.

Even as the Anthropocene extends its purview over geology within an explicitly politicized optic on geomorphic processes, it is a "view from nowhere." The God's-eye view is inverted into a lithic-eye view to produce a geologic commons from below (Yusoff 2017b). The unification of its vision across the time and space of geologic practices seemingly offers an undifferentiating and indifferent politic. Apprehending the past in the present colonial mining empires of white settler nations frames White Geology as a historical regime of material power, not a genetic imaginary. In this book, I want to redress how the descriptive qualities of geology's nomenclature produce what Hartman calls a "cultivated silence" about the normalcy of those extractive modes as deracialized. To address this silence would be to understand geology as a regime for producing both subjects and material worlds, where race is established as an effect of power within the language of geology's objects. Specifically, the border in the division of materiality (and its subjects) as inhuman and human, and thus as inert or agentic matter, operationalizes race.

White Geology makes legible a set of extractions, from particular subject positions, from black and brown bodies, and from the ecologies of place. The collective functioning of geologic languages coded—inhuman, property, value, possession— as categories moves across territory, relation, and flesh. It is not just that geology is a signifier for extraction but that a transmutation of matter occurs within that signification that renders matter as property, that makes a delineation between agency and inertness, which stabilizes the *cut* of property and enacts the removal of matter from its constitutive relations as both subject and mineral embedded in sociological and ecological fields. Thus I argue that the semiotics of White Geology creates *a*temporal materiality dislocated from place and time—a mythology of disassociation in the formation of matter independent of its languages of description and the historical constitution of its social relations.

The division between the figures of the human and inhuman and its manifestations in subjective life exhibits one of the most terrible consequences of the division of materiality organized and practiced as a biopolitical tool of governance. The division of matter into nonlife and life pertains not only to matter but to the racial organization of life as foundational to New World geographies. The biopolitical category of nonbeing is established through slaves being exchanged for and as gold. Slavery was a geologic axiom of the inhuman in which nonbeing was made, reproduced, and circulated as flesh. This unmaking of subjects constitutes a warp of dispossession in the progressive narrative of collective accumulation or geologic commons in which "we" all share. The rendering of nonbeings in colonial extractive practices through the designation of inhuman or geologic life, its exchange and circulation, demonstrates what Christina Sharp (2009) calls the "monstrous intimacy" of the subjective powers of geology, where gold shows up as bodies and bodies are the surplus of mineralogical extraction. The inhuman is a call across categories, material and symbolic, corporeal and incorporeal, intimacies cut across life and nonlife in the indifferent register of matter.

Geology (and its fossil objects) have been entwined with questions of origins, processes of racialization through speciation and notions of progress, as well as being a praxis for inscripting racial logics *within* the material politics of extraction that constitutes lived forms of racism (from eugenics to environmental racism). To trace racial matterings across the category of the inhuman, and specifically the traffic between the *inhuman as matter* and the *inhuman as race,* is to examine how the concept of the inhuman is a connective hinge in the twinned discourses of geology and humanism. It is a hinge that establishes an extractive axis in both subjective and geologic (or planetary) life. Race (and the Human) is tied most noticeably to fossil narratives (Yusoff 2013, 2016) and racialized processes of extraction, but it is also resident in modes of racial discourse in relation to ideas of property, possession, and land use. In the categorization of matter as *property* and *properties,* both spatial dispossession of land (for extraction) and dispossessions of persons in chattel slavery (as another form of spatial extraction) are enacted. The slave in this formulation is rendered as matter, recognized through an inhuman property relation—what Saidiya Hartman calls fungibility—as a commodity with properties, but without subjective will or agency (or "flesh," as Hortense Spiller has it). Rendering subjects as inhuman matter, not as persons, thereby facilitated and incorporated the historical fact of extraction of personhood as a quality of geology at its inception.

Following the work of Hartman and Spillers, I want to pay attention to the grammars of geology and to think with the modes of objectification that the genre of the Anthropocene both unleashes and maintains. This material language of the inhuman and its production of the subjective category of nonbeing set up historical deformations and present impossibilities for subjective life, specifically in what Hartman (1997) calls the "afterlives of slavery." The mine and the afterlives of its geomorphic acts constitute the materiality of the Anthropocene and its natal moment, from the transformation of mineralogy of the earth in the extraction of gold, silver, salt, and copper to the massive transformation of ecologies in the movement of people, plants, and animals across territories, coupled with the intensive implantation of monocultures of indigo, sugar, tobacco, cotton, and other "alien" ecologies in the New World. The complex histories of those afterlives of slavery continued in the chain gangs that laid the railroad and worked the coal mines through to the establishment of new forms of energy, in which, Stephanie LeMenager (2014, 5) comments, "oil literally was conceived as a replacement for slave labor." Approaching race as a geologic proposition (or *geologies of race*) is a way, then, to open up the imbrication of inhuman materials and relations of extraction that go beyond a place-based configuration of environmental racism as a spatial organization of exposure to environmental harm. There is a need to examine the epistemological framings and categorizations that produce the material and discursive world building through geology in both its historical and present forms. Specifically, in the lexicon of geology—as a naming of property and properties—certain extractive modes are configured and deployed to enact dispossession across territorial and subjective registers. Geology is historically situated as a *transactional zone* in which propertied and proprietorial concepts of self are entangled—as the entanglement of slavery versus freedom and the material forms of social subjective life versus liberal individuation.

If the first stake at redressing political geology is to call for the disruption of the connotative powers of language—the exchangeability between human and thing, subject and matter—then the second is to follow this suspension with an orientation that acknowledges the afterlife of this disruption as an ongoing struggle of reorientation in valuing black life and in concomitant struggles for uncontaminated water, air, and land. Why is it that the language of geology allows for the exchange of a person as a material object of property and properties (a unit of corporeal energy), and how does it bypass established biopolitical registers of critique? What are the psychic figurations of gold and slave in the colonial cartographic imagination that allow this symbolic and material exchange? The resolution of this interchangeability happens in the geologic language of the inhuman and the lexicons of inert and nonagentic matter. My intention is not to reclaim the inhuman as a dialectical position from which to reframe humanist exclusions in relation to their Others (because, as Wynter reminds us, the Human is an occupied category); rather, I want to think with the inhuman as an analytic with which to scrutinize the traffic between relations of race and material economy and to think race as a material economy that itself emerges through the libidinal economy of geology (as the desire for gold, mineralogy, and metallurgy). But what are the relays involved between the classifications of geology and the classifications of race? How does slavery function as an inhuman "category mistake" (Spillers 2003, 20) of geology? Between mineral-as-property and person-as-property, after

Spillers, "the question for me remains the concatenation itself—what in the nature of 'property' might have provoked a sufficient enough displacement and condensation along a sequence of analogical thinking that would bring it within the scope of 'human'" (Spillers 2003, 20)?

Addressing the racialization of geology within the context of the new origin stories that are being fashioned in the search for the beginning of the Anthropocene epoch, I think with the historicity that is being structured into these events—what Dionne Brand (2017a) calls the "corpses of the humanist narrative" that constitute the sedimented "nonevent" of those moments. This subjective and subjugating geologic life happens in the fugitive or insurgent space-time of Anthropocenic geology, yet it is the very quotidian practices that constitute it and are constituting of subjects. This is to see the Anthropocene as a psychopolitical staging of subjectivity as well as a historical rendering of materiality (Yusoff 2015). If this project seems like a counterhistory of geologic relations that is other to current articulation as a linear narrative of accumulation, then mine is certainly an attempt to open an investigation into that history and to the languages that carry the work of geology in the world (as resource, extraction, inhuman, chattel). The birth of a geologic subject in the Anthropocene made without an examination of this history is a deadly erasure, rebirth without responsibility.

The revisiting of origin stories in the Anthropocene also contains a broader question: what are the encroachments on subjective life that take place through geology and its description of materiality? Another way to put this would be to ask, how does the maintenance of structures of materiality (or geologic codes) facilitate and perpetuate antiblackness and its forms of subjugation, as well as ongoing settler colonialism? How is geology an operation of power, as well as a temporal explanation for life on the planet? And what are the intimate contours of its material possessions (as property and extraction)? The exercise of power is not simply explained in terms of how slavery engendered racialized subjects as objects but also within the language of geology itself, which allowed such traversals to be made in the first instance. The language of materiality and its division between life and nonlife, and its alignment with concepts of the human and inhuman, facilitated the divisions between subjects as humans and subjects priced as flesh (or inhuman matter).

While the human and inhuman are so often mapped as binaries onto organic and inorganic matter and its descriptions, as dialectics or defining modes, there is an *infra*materialism that often slips out of view in the perceived autonomism of these states of matter that are rendered as either biology or geology. Put differently, geology is often assumed to be without a subject (thinglike and inert), whereas biology is secured in the recognition of the organism (bodylike and sentient). Thinking Blackness in terms of the relations of materiality, of coal black, black gold, black metal, and how these are configured in discourses of geology and its lexicons of matter uncovers the transactions between geology and inhumanism as a mode of both production (or extraction) and subjection (or a violent mode of geologic life). How do Blackness and the terminology of geology slip into each other as equivalent substances? How is such an alchemy of slavery and geology possible? How is geology as a discipline and extraction process cooked together in the crucible of slavery and colonialism? How does this geology (as a colonial and neocolonial strategy) enact territorial extraction (through survey, classification, codification, and annexation)?

Following these lines of inquiry gives rise to questions about agency and consent, around sentience and inhuman matter, and how material agency with and without subjectivity is thought outside of the structures of cozy humanism and its languages of existence. As Édouard Glissant (2010, xi) makes clear, "I build my language with rocks." Dionne Brand (1996, 76) similarly writes, "I want to go against the ground, grind it in my teeth, but most I want to plunge my hands in stone." The history of Blackness by its very negation in the category of nonbeing within economies of Whiteness lives differently in the earth, where "blackness is defined here in terms of social relationality rather than identity" (Hartman 1997, 56)—a relation realized in a different material register as "an aesthetics of disruption and intrusion . . . aesthetics of rupture and connection" (Glissant 1997, 151). In this aesthetics of the earth, Glissant identifies the crux of the problem as the transformation of land into territory: "Territory is the basis for conquest. Territory requires filiation to be planted and legitimated. Territory is defined by its limits, and they must be expanded" (151). In an act of intrusion, I seek to undermine the *givenness* of geology as an innocent or natural description of the world, to see its modes of inscription and circulation as a doubling of the notion of property—property as a description of mineralogy and property as an acquisition (as resource, land, extractive quality of energy or mineral). This geologic lexicon is a practice that enacts colonialism through what Sylvia Wynter called "scientific humanism" that is mobilized as a praxis for dispossession.

The epistemological divisions of geology and biology and their respective analytics of geopolitics and biopolitics divide the world between the skein of biopolitical coercion and territorial arrangements of populations, leaving the interaction between the geopolitical and biopolitical worlds as a problem of how the politics of scale meshes into subjective life. This epistemic division sediments a geologic that was necessary for colonial theft, because it allowed slaves to turn into and displace gold and refused to acknowledge indigenous relations with "dead" matter. For example, the Gold Coast as a source of both gold and slaves was itself referred to as "the Mine" (Hartman 2007, 51). These relations found their neocolonial afterlives in the extraction industries of former colonies. (For example, the British platinum mine on the Bushveld Igneous Complex authorized attacks by police and security services in 2012 on striking miners, leaving thirty-four miners dead.) Geology is a relation of power and continues to constitute racialized relations of power, in its incarnation in the Anthropocene and in its material manifestation in mining, petrochemical sites and corridors, and their toxic legacies— all over a world that resolutely cuts exposure along color lines.

While attention has been paid to the role of scientific epistemes in the modern formation of race through colonization and enslavement stretching across an epoch of imperial world building that is not yet at its end, the historic subject (as European-Human and its Others) is conceived of as a biologic, not a geologic, subject. As Elizabeth Povinelli (2016) comments, the dominant mode of subjectivity of late liberalism is of the biocentric subject. There is an obscurity or opacity accorded to geopolitical affects at the level of the subject formations that exceeds the territorial impositions of biopolitical orderings. By that, I mean that the geophysics of being has been neglected in accounts of colonial violence. The intimacy of this geophysics as an experiential and structural form of (geologic) life enacts sensibilities of matter, time, gravity, mud, and weather as inhabitations that are absent from the geospatial confinements of these geopolitics. Christina Sharpe (2016a, 134) says, "So we are here in the weather, here in the singularity. Here there is disaster and possibility. And while *'we are constituted through and by continued vulnerability to this overwhelming force, we are not only known to ourselves and to each other by that force'*" (quoting Brand, emphasis original). These counterhistories are found elsewhere in the narratives and scenes of subjection, in excess of the complicated matrixes of colonial life, in literature and music—not as expressions of those geopolitics but as a tactical theoretical response that remakes subjectivity through the senses as a concrete analytic. Wynter (n.d., 109) suggests that the axiomatic torque of sensibility is made in provisional ground, "where the mind feels and the senses become theoreticians." This geophysics of being within the Empire of Geology finds its trace and place in critical black aesthetics.

Monuments to Geologic Reason and Provisional Ground

Seeking to monumentalize Anthropocene history is an attempt to reclaim an "innocence" around this geohistory. The histories of the Anthropocene unfold a brutal experience for much of the world's racialized poor and without due attention to the historicity of those events (and their eventfulness); the Anthropocene simply consolidates power via this innocence in the present to effect decisions that are made about the future and its modes of survival. The sleight of hand of the Janus-faced discipline of geology (as extractive economy and deep-time paleontology of lifeforms) is to naturalize (and thus neutralize) the theft of extraction through its grammars of extraction. Recast as "development," the colonial and settler-colonial dispossession of the relation to land and geography was never something chosen without coercion. So, monuments made to these moments of extraction only accrue the extension of value to those colonial forces. To be included in the "we" of the Anthropocene is to be silenced by a claim to universalism that fails to notice its subjugations, taking part in a planetary condition in *which no part* was accorded in terms of subjectivity. The supposed "we" further legitimates and justifies the racialized inequalities that are bound up in social geologies.

My aim in this book is to make a narrative that refuses this account of the earth and its subjects as units of economic extraction, while launching a conversation about how political geology might look otherwise. The attachment to writing with and against a social geology is not to "humanize" geology so much as it is to understand how the languages that already reside within it are mobilized as relations of power—and how a different economy of description might give rise to a more exacting understanding of geologic materiality that is less deadly (by refusing the routine brutalities of economies of extraction and the legacy of colonial asset-making practices through geology). Thinking of the Anthropocene as a set of material practices of duration and arrival that brought this world into being, alongside the fact that for a certain proportion of the world, the entire dismantling of this colonial apparatus is a desired state, launches a call for a different kind of world making. As the science fiction writer N. K. Jemisin and Hartman point out in the epigraphs at the beginning of this chapter, the end of this world has already happened for some subjects, and it is the prerequisite for the possibility of imagining "living and breathing again" for others. If the Anthropocene is delivering a new geochemical earth through the excess of colonial practices, then it is not just the geophysical processes that need attention but the whole history of world making as a geophysics of being—a world making that was for the few and firmly committed to the enlightenment project of liberal individualism and its exclusions. The social life of geology, then, is not a biographical account of geology but a praxis, a world making in the present, in light of the inheritances of past geosocial formations. In the blocked horizon of the Anthropocene in which geology emerges as an end-game negotiation with the planet and late liberalism, geology can finally be recognized as a regime for producing subjects and regulating subjective lives—a place where the properties of belonging are negotiated.

Anthropocene monumentality is a way to unpack the language that geology carries and a way to push a conversation that admonishes the idea of the neutrality of geology as a language of the rocks and deep time, which is immune or innocent of its current deadly configurations. What often becomes "political" in geologic relations is infrastructure—mine, pipeline, coal field, water rights, land dispossession, namely, material political economy. And these infrastructures are embedded in important fights, which show up a network of power relations and subordinations (such as the Dakota Access Pipeline), but there is also a prior economy of power, a historical geography of the discipline and its functioning (as academic formation and applied material economy) that is preconfigured through a racialized geosocial matrix. If we abandon the absurd notion that geology is somehow immune from the violence and dispossession enacted through extraction of mineral resources, then geology in its fully geosocial registers comes to the fore as a force of transformation.[2]

2. It should be noted that the only reason we know anything about geology is because of fossils uncovered through mining and the motivation for the development of geologic knowledge in order to mobilize this extraction frame.

What I am proposing is that geology is a racialized optic razed on the earth. While the connection between geology and life is being recognized at all manner of biological, chemical and geomorphic scales under the rubric of the Anthropocene, the intimate contours of geologic life as a force and power with subjective life remain decisively mute (Yusoff 2016, 2017b). Naming can also be a covering over. The Anthropocene is a retooling of geology, from a discipline of extractive and originary science to a philosophical material formation. If the Anthropocene is retooling geology, there is a need to retool the Anthropocene precisely because of how these territorial histories are tethered to racializing matter. To move to substantiate the geomateriality of race is to attempt to locate a disposition and position in the Anthropocene that negates the invisible work of social reproduction in material relations, which is the antiblack directionality of extraction and ongoing settler colonialism.

It might be easier to contend that race is not a "problem" of geology but a problem of humanism and *its* exclusions; blame the master, not the tools. But geology is more than a tool; it is a technology of matter, its formulation and the desire that shapes its incarnation. Initiating the Atlantic slave trade in the protocapitalist moment of 1441, the first slaves sold in Lisbon, Portugal, were conceived of as slaves within the "problem" of mining in Brazil: the perceived difficulties of indigenous labor (given that 90 percent of the population was wiped out due to violence and disease) and the properties that were imagined to reside in black flesh on the Gold Coast. This act establishes the first color line of White Geology. The solution of race becomes enfolded in geology as a material technology of extraction, and the semiotics of race become inscripted in geological modes of classification *as* a matter relation. Often the analysis for slavery begins with the question of labor, which makes sense, up until a point, but there is a desire that launches that point into existence, that prompts the question, of labor for what? At this point, we arrive at the explanation of the plantations, the sugar in the bowl, and the cotton that needed picking, but before these precapitalist economies there was the gold, silver, and copper mining that mobilized the *hunger* for the slavery, and later, the sugar, that fueled the English working classes of the Industrial Revolution in their extraction of coal (see Mintz 1985). As Césaire ([1956] 1969, 61) writes, "we are walking compost hideously promising tender cane and silky cotton." In the nonconsensual collaboration with inhuman materiality as both a property of energy and in concert with other energy sources (sugar, coal, mineral), slavery weaponized the redistribution of energy around the globe through the flesh of black bodies.

As the largest forced migration of people in the world, the profits accrued from the enslaved during the transatlantic slave trade laid the economic foundation for Western Europe, the Caribbean, and the Americas. As text in the National Museum of African American History and Culture (NMAAHC, in Washington, D.C.) bids us remember about the intimacies of these material relations, "the human cost was the immense physical and psychological toll on the enslaved. Their lives were embedded in every coin that changed hands, each spoonful of sugar stirred into a cup of tea, each puff of a pipe, and every bite of rice." That the massive increase in sugar consumption in 1850 maps directly onto the massive increase in coal use is perhaps not surprising, as sugar was the conversion of inhumane slave energy into fuel, then back into human energy, plus inhuman energy, to produce industrialization. Coal was the inhuman corollary of those dehumanized black bodies. Coal black. Yet, histories of the Anthropocene ubiquitously begin with meditations on the great white men of industry and innovation to reinforce imperial genealogies. For example, "global warming is the unintended by-product par excellence. A cotton manufacturer of early nineteenth-century Lancashire who decided to forgo his old waterwheel and invest in a steam engine, erect a chimney and order coal from a nearby pit did not, in all likelihood, entertain the possibility that this act could have any kind of relationship to the extent of Arctic sea ice, the salinity of Nile Delta soil, the altitude of the Maldives, the frequency of droughts on the Horn of Africa"

(Malm 2015, 1). But why did the manufacturer not pause, if not to consider global warming, then to consider the other "unintended by-products" of cotton manufacturing? Why did the author not even take the presence of cotton in the second line of his introduction to the book to be alerted to the clamor and rattling of chains? In the cast of white men who shaped the world, why did cotton not even "signal" another geography to this narrative of white bibliography? Why did he locate his project in the imperial–colonial narrative tropes of character, place, and agency? Isn't this over-writing of the nonbeing or excess of the inhuman and inhumanity the very issue that is at stake in the "unintended by-product"? As James Baldwin and Margaret Mead (1971, 177) suggest, "what we call history is perhaps a way of avoiding responsibility for what has happened, is happening, in time."

The movement of energy between enslaved bodies in plantations, plants, long-dead fossilized plants, and industrialized labor is a geochemical equation of extraction in the conversion of surplus. But this racialized equation of energy is located in a larger field of production and semiotics of extraction. Slavery is not a by-product of this process; rather, slavery is driven by an indifferent extractive geo-logic that is motivated by the desire for inhuman properties. Indigenous genocide and settler colonialism are also part of these extractive geo-logics. In this sense, slavery can be seen not as a confusion of subject–object in relation to inhuman categorization but as a total submission to the principle of extraction that was exacted through inhuman differentiation—"transformed from the *human subject* of his own culture into the *inhuman object* of the European culture" (Wynter, n.d., 10, emphasis original). The energy regimes that structure material extraction were forced into black material and psychic life—of being energy for others, of putting sugar in the bowl, and in the muscles of white labor; as an "object" of geochemical energy and the rationalization of the black body; as energetic pleasure in all its myriad forms that render the "open and absolute vulnerability" (Sexton 2010, 44) of black and brown bodies to white extraction regimes. This intervention is the beginning of asking about the process by which such exchanges become possible.

Note on Erasure

The tense of this work and the impetus for its writing came out of a repeated positioning within the white spaces of Anthropocene academic events and as a response to the lack of recognition of race within those places. The "extreme discretion of the scholarly community" (Hartman 2002, 771) in its decision not to engage with race and settler colonialism most clearly refuted the critical claims being made about the Anthropocene. More than the ubiquitous social typology of dominant white men in the academy, it was the question of the very Whiteness of geology itself as a material practice that snagged for me. The development of an analytic of White Geology is important for how the Anthropocene is conceived, in terms of its origin stories and an environmental relation to come (beyond liberal individuation). The persistent discomfort with comfortable exclusions meant that this work started as a redress, writing toward a darker Anthropocene—the underbelly of White Geology—but this seemed to leave the institutional structures of the "event" of geology (and the language that it carried) firmly intact. Understanding Blackness not as metaphor but as materiality (that has a symbolic, territorial, and psychic life), the second part of the book expands and undercuts the "events" of settler colonialism and anti-Blackness that are being monumentalized in Golden Spikes. Hartman reminds the reader at the onset of her seminal book *Scenes of Subjection* of the all-too-familiar and reproducible "spectacular character of black suffering" (3), and it is my intention here, at the caution of many black studies scholars, not to reproduce the genre of black (social) death through geologic means. I do want to acknowledge, however, how the praxis of geology was used as an instrument of deformation in the possibilities of collective subjective and ecological life for black and brown communities.

It would be straightforward, perhaps, to "fill out" the Anthropocene through the dark context of its origin stories, but that would not repudiate the structures of thought and material arrangements that brought the Anthropocene into being in the first place. Work in black and indigenous studies[3] is critical in this context precisely because it articulates intimate confinements and ongoing containments of humanist thought, while simultaneously calling for a reconfiguring of possibilities of subjective experience. Furthermore, the exclusion of black and brown subjects from the humanist master-subject and its ties to geographical dispossession (in genocide, natal alienation, and ongoing environmental racism) has forged a rearrangement of the structures and sounds of materiality in black and indigenous experience. If the Anthropocene is viewed as a resurrection of the impulse to reestablish humanism in all its exclusionary terms of universality, then any critical theory that does not work with and alongside black and indigenous studies (rather than in an extractive or supplementary mode) will fail to deliver any epochal shift at all. It would be in Césaire's words in the epigraph to the book, to think the "thought of the other" without the "other of thought."

The hope for this work is to orient toward a less coercive geology through the critique and expansion of its grammars. The problem of race has been posed precisely as the problem of the human (that is, the figure of humanism). But if we were to start with the prefiguration of the human, in its inception within the technologies of the inhuman, a different model of extraction would emerge. To put it another way, if the human is but one of the problems of redress in colonialism, which, regardless of attempts at negotiation, will remain an exclusive subjectivity in terms of both its designation of rights (Wynter 2015; Bogue 2006) and the possibility

3. The fields of indigenous studies and black studies are complex in their differences and their exactitude of cojoined but differently enacted historical experience, especially in the context of natality and genealogies of land rights.

of empathy or reciprocity (Hartman 2007; Wilderston 2008), then starting with the category of the inhuman liberates the possibility of a redescription of relation that can "take place and have a place" (McKittrick 2011). In a corollary to geology's inhuman/inhumane modes of description, black poetics is epoch making in its redirection of the racial logics of extraction through new energetic modes and understandings of relation, desedimenting the forms of inhuman historicity that are established through colonialism. Hartman comments that these practices and poetics forged in the terror of slavery were necessarily subterranean: "For this opacity, the subterranean and veiled character of slave song must be considered in relation to the dominant imposition of transparency and the degrading hypervisibility of the enslaved, and therefore, by the same token, such concealment should be considered a form of resistance" (Hartman 2007, 36). In the forced alliances with the inhuman, a different mode of subjective relation is forged, where Blackness is a name for nonnormative subjectivity (Moten 2003, 2016) or, in Césaire's ([1972] 2000, 55) words, a "communistic materialism."

Origin Stories for a New Epoch

The first part of this book, "Golden Spikes and Dubious Origins," concentrates on the origin stories of the Anthropocene, the so-called Golden Spikes of geology, where a ubiquitous planetary mark in the strata consecrates the epochal shift. In this political stratigraphy, I trace the historiography of Colonial Man to Anthropocene Man to frame the so-called Geology of Mankind as a privileged subjective space. Then, by looking at the originary stories of the Anthropocene—1610 Columbian "exchange"; 1800s industrialization; 1950s Great Acceleration—I argue how coloniality and anti-Blackness are materially inscribed into the Anthropocene. Material stories are origin stories—stories that reproduce not just arrangements of matter but subjects through divisions of matter. This formation of geologic origination is important to consider in the construction of the Anthropocene in both narrative and material domains precisely because of the power of stories to designate scenes of agency and accountability. Colonial strategies of occupation have long concentrated on genealogy to identify (and thus coerce) existing political authority and to identify an anthropology of "Otherness" that marks the colonized through a divisive cut of difference (which in turn justified theft of territory and persons).[4] And, beyond this recognition of the power of origin stories and their hold on the present, there is a need to register the aesthetic–symbolic qualities of oppression as a mode of categorization that is already implicated in the organization of subjective lives through geology.

The subsequent chapter, "The Inhumanities," locates the historic work of geology in the racialization of matter through slavery and histories of geologic surveying in the establishing settler colonialism. Starting with Charles Lyell's speculations on geology and slavery in his 1845 *Travels in North America,* I discuss these entwined scenes to show how the organization and categorization of matter enact racialization. This enactment is productive of both *a racial logics* that extends through and beyond mineralogy and a *deterritorialization* that accompanies extraction. Geology provides the geo-logics to elide those attachments through its classification system of value and resource, while slavery leaves subjects marooned and captured in the indices of the inhuman. This chapter addresses how the social formation of geology through modes of classification, ordering, and representation is a mattering grid

---

4. For example, while writing up this work on an Advanced Institute Fellowship at Durham University, we had a tour of the Palace Green library, where substantial archives on the British colony on Sudan are kept. In this colonial archive were maps of relations between tribes and attempts to decipher their genealogy to establish a cartography of authority. This was complemented by anthropology reports on tribal markings, earth eaters, tattooing, female circumcision, and native surgery (Sudan 1908), in an attempt to decipher markers of sexuality and rites and rituals that produced the native as other.

of colonialism or a taxonomy of race. I suggest that there is a tight material rapport between the designation and organization of the inhuman as mineralogy/geology and the inhumane that is established via an attachment to liberal humanism (and its reincarnation in Anthropocene discourses).

The next chapter, "Insurgent Geology: A Billion Black Anthropocenes Now," opens up questions about the flesh of the Anthropocene that were raised in the previous chapters through its origin stories and (in)humanist frames. It seeks to take apart the construction of the "event" of geology by staging an engagement with slavery and subjugation, and rather than overwriting nonbeing (again), I follow Caribbean and diaspora writers into the wake, weather, and alluvial mud of colonial dissipation to explore the silenced archives of geologic acts. Specifically, this chapter engages with Sylvia Wynter's unpublished manuscript "Black Metamorphosis," in which she attends to the "metamorphosis by which the multi-tribal African became the native of that area of experience that we term the New World" or the process of *trans*plantation (as she terms it) (Wynter, n.d., 2). Finally, I follow recent critical moves in black aesthetics to question how starting with the "End of the World" might release a more exacting critique of this geologic epoch and its material registers of being, liberated from liberal subjectivity into an alternate geophysics of being by a reworking of gravity.

In moving toward the idea of a billion Black Anthropocenes, I am not advocating that indigenous and colonized peoples' knowledge practices be mobilized as an experimental outside or supplement to Western scientific knowledge practices. Rather, I want to suggest that race, following Silva (2007), might be considered as foundational to the production of Global-World-Space and geologic regimes of governance that become manifest in the practices of White Geology (or the Anthropocene). Bearing in mind Toni Morrison's (1992, x) caution against the "metaphoric shortcuts" in relation to Blackness, in which she urges a recognition of "language that can powerfully evoke and enforce hidden signs of racial superiority, cultural hegemony, and dismissive 'othering' of people and language," addressing origin stories is not just about making an alternative or alt-anthro-scene. Rather, it is to be attentive to what histories of the earth provide a break in analysis and narratives of material relations and languages of description that have colonized it, and to begin to make histories that launch a praxis for an insurgent geology into being—an insurgent geology that is, to paraphrase Brand, flooded with the world. This is where materiality is used to establish the presentness of Blackness as an obligation to the present, to counter its erasure through a poetry that cuts into coloniality as counteraesthetic (Brand 2017b). To this end, I write not toward White Geology but toward the "nonevent" of a billion Black Anthropocenes.

I must begin.
Begin what?
The only thing in the world that's worth beginning:
The End of the World, no less (Césaire [1956] 1969, 39)

Golden Spikes and Dubious Origins

Too much has been made of origins. All origins are arbitrary.
This is not to say that they are not also nurturing, but they are
essentially coercive and indifferent

—DIONNE BRAND, *A Map to the Door of No Return: Notes to Belonging*

The white utopia was black inferno.

—SYLVIA WYNTER, "Unsettling the Coloniality of Being/
Power/Truth/Freedom: Toward the Human, After Man, Its
Overrepresentation—An Argument," *The New Centennial Review*

The Fabulation of Beginnings

As the Anthropocene signals alarm bells over human–planetary
ends, the search is under way for its beginnings. To be established
as an epoch, the Anthropocene must be tethered to an origin that
confirms "you are Here" in the Age of Humans. In the discourse
that surrounds the empirics of fossil traces, foundational myths of
how and why "we" got here are being instigated. But this "we" cannot be immune to who is writing and mobilizing this history and
the implications of its telling for who is granted agency in shaping
the present and future. While the search for the Golden Spike is a
disciplinary endeavor to geologically map the material relation of
space and time according to stratigraphic principles and scientific
precedents, these spikes are not real places as such; they are trace

effects in material worlds that infer the event/advent of this most political geology. In this chapter, I want to draw attention to the interlinked material and conceptual architectures of slavery and industrialization and their interlocutors, humanism and race, to argue that geologic origin stories function as identity politics that coheres around an exclusive notion of humanity (coded white). I start by examining the fabulation of beginnings in the quest for the Golden Spike as prologue to a discussion about who gets spiked by geology (or, what color is the flesh of geology?).

The scientific community offer us three possible material beginnings for the Anthropocene subject: the Columbian "exchange" and "Orbis hypothesis" event (Lewis and Maslin 2015) (1610); the Industrial Revolution and James Watt's steam engine (1800); and the "Great Acceleration" and nuclear isotopes from missile testing. Although only informally added to the chronostratigraphic chart, the Anthropocene Working Group (AWG) delivered its findings to the thirty-fifth International Geological Congress in South Africa in 2017, and a boundary marker, or Golden Spike, will likely be agreed upon in the coming years (although there is much disagreement over what constitutes a proper boundary marker). In other words, although origins structure the axis of geological time, they are not immune to the narrative overtures that trouble questions of origination elsewhere in political geography. Graphia of rock is no less subject to world building than attempts to calcify origins in projects of nationalism. Origins draw borders that define inclusion and exclusion, and their focus is narrow, narrating a line of purpose (read Progress) and purposefulness (read Civilization), while overlooking accident, misdirection, or the shadow geology of disposable lives, waste, toxicity, contamination, extinction, and exhaustion. There is not geology on one hand and stories about geology on the other; rather, there is an axis of power and performance that meets within these geologic objects and the narratives they tell about the human story. Traveling back and forth through materiality and narrative, the origins of the Anthropocene are intensely political in how they draw the world of the present into being and give shape and race to its world-making subjects.

This chapter focuses on the three moments of "Anthropogenesis" that are under consideration by the International Commission on Stratigraphy to unearth these monuments. Elsewhere, I use the term *Anthropogenesis* (Yusoff 2016) to refer to how materiality takes on an originary status in the Anthropocene; origins constitute and conjoin the site and subjective life of the Anthropocene through a geologic marker that pronounces the threshold event of becoming a geologic agent of the planet. The anthropocentrism of the Anthropocene is a world-making practice, nominating "1) the production of a mythic Anthropos as geologic worldmaker/destroyer of worlds, and 2) a material, evolutionary narrative that re-imagines human origins and endings within a geologic rather than an exclusively biological context" (Yusoff 2016, 3). In this ascension to geologic force, the Anthropocene creates a planetary genesis that ties the *Anthropos* to the creation of an epoch, substituting human agency for geologic processes. Thereby geology is designated as a subjective mode of the human *and* a universal model of material agency that has inadvertently assumed mastery over geologic processes. The sedimentation of this force of geology into subjective life is both material and semantic. As Derrida would have it, nothing that can be found in the end is not already prefigured in the origin. Origins configure and prefigure the possibility of narratives of the present: the Anthropocene-in-the-making. Origination of the event of this geologic happening organizes a material and discursive space that arranges relations of power through the constitution of beginnings and ends that reproduce formations of power in the present through an account of materialities of the past.

As a mineralogical punctuation event in geologic processes, the Anthropocene names an empire that is not yet at its end, and so any account of the gravity and tense of that trajectory accounts for, and reorganizes, understandings of ongoing geosocial processes. Origins, then, are another word for an account of agency or a trajectory of power. Geology is a transactional zone in which ideas of origins, subjectivity, and matter are intertwined, with historical materialist roots that span a genealogy of dispossession, uprooting, and extreme violence. In thinking about geology as an intensely extractive praxis, there is a need to question what Eve Tuck and K. Wayne Yang (2012, 1) call settler "moves to innocence" in the claims about the newly found consciousness that permeates Anthropocenic scientific and social scientific discourse. This is the claim that humanity has failed to understand the violent repercussions of colonialism, industrialization, or capitalist modes of production and that these violences were an unforeseen by-product or excess of these practices and not a central tenet of them. Aptly, capturing the geomatrix of racial formations and land dispossession under colonialism, W. E. B. Du Bois (1920, 54) defined Whiteness as the "ownership of the Earth for ever and ever." Taking seriously the future perfect tense of White Geology forces a consideration of *where* violence is located in geologic practices and its modes of recognition (as geologic "event" and subjective marks). The Anthropocenic "history lesson" in which humanity undergoes a sudden realization of the violent and repressive dimensions of coloniality and then, in the eclipse of modernity, puts these violences firmly in the past, while continuing to perpetuate them through an ongoing settler-colonial present, can be seen in this example from Paul Crutzen and Christian Schwäger (2011):

> To master this huge shift, we must change the way we perceive ourselves and our role in the world. Students in school are still taught that we are living in the Holocene, an era that began roughly 12,000 years ago at the end of the last Ice Age. But teaching students that we are living in the Anthropocene, the Age of Men, could be of great help. Rather than representing yet another sign of human hubris, this name change would stress the enormity of humanity's responsibility as stewards of the Earth. It would highlight the *immense power of our intellect and our creativity*, and the opportunities they offer for shaping the future. . . . The awareness of living in the *Age of Men* could inject some desperately needed eco-optimism into our societies. . . . With countries worldwide striving to attain the *"American Way of Life," citizens of the West* should redefine it—and *pioneer* a

modest, renewable, mindful, and less material lifestyle. . . . *We* also
need to develop geoengineering capabilities in order to be prepared
for worst-case scenarios. (emphasis added)

This attempt to absolve the positionality of Western colonial
knowledge and extraction practices, while simultaneously reinforcing and resettling them in a new territory—a Western frontier of pioneers armed with eco-optimism and geoengineering—
indicates a desire to overcome coloniality without a corresponding
relinquishing of the power it continues to generate in terms of
who gets to formulate, implement, and speak to/of the future. In
this imagination of humanity, the heirs of an "American Way of
Life" (or white reproductive settler colonialism) structure a col-
or line of agency. Notwithstanding the references to frontierism,
Western modernity, and the "citizens of the West" as the guaran-
tors of intellect and creativity, the epochal sea change that is imagined actually reinstates the same old story of dominion, articulated through Judeo-Christian stewardship of Empire. The colonial
assumption for the responsibility for and of the world is articulated anew as the white man's burden—a paternalism that is tied to
a redemptive narrative of saving the world from harm on account
of others while maintaining the protective thick skin of innocence.

What Crutzen and Schwäger (2011) do so expertly is to nar-
rate the imagined steps toward progress and triumph over
Anthropocenic conditions that are already secreted within these
discursive formations. While Crutzen (2002, 23) himself notes
that "these effects have largely been caused by only 25% of the
world population," his assumption of "responsibility" (and thus
agency, in the formulation of origins = agency) is misplaced. It is
a false evolutionism that designates a single point of experience
from which departure for the future is projected. As Brand (2001,
82) reminds us, there is no ground zero in relation; "it never occurs to them that they live on the cumulative hurt of others. They
want to start the clock of social justice only when they arrive. But
one is born into history, one isn't born into a void." Right behind

claims of naming, interpretation, and description come the proposal of solutions and the delimitation of scenes of power. Crutzen presents us with a contrite Western civilization that, despite the obvious repressed excesses of its geologic formations—named the Anthropocene—continues to devise hegemonic aspirations that deny both those subjective repressions and the multisovereignties they represent. Those histories of black and brown Undercommons (Moten and Harney 2013) are contorted into an oversight of civilization, as are the environmental effects of colonialism and industrialization, making way for a present that continues to privilege the privileged. The solutions and proposals are all about the continuance of the current stasis of inequality, powered by other means. In this telling, the Anthropocene is white man's overburden.[1]

Material Markers; or, *What* and *Who* Get Marked in Anthropocene Origin Stories

A formal geologic unit of time requires a global stratotype section and point or a Golden Spike in the strata, plus other stratigraphic markers that indicate long-term shifts in the earth system to mark the boundary. As a geologic event, the Anthropocene is unusual insomuch as it does not present the usual millions of years to achieve its geologic swerve but must rely on decadal or century scales. As a stratigraphic event, the Anthropocene represents a compression of geologic time. As Lewis and Maslin (2015, 171) make clear,

> unlike other geological time unit designations, definitions will probably have effects beyond geology. For example, defining an early start date may, in political terms, "normalize" global environmental change. Meanwhile, agreeing [on] a later start date related to the Industrial Revolution may, for example, be used to assign historical responsibility for carbon dioxide emissions to particular countries or regions during the industrial era. More broadly, the formal definition

---

1. Thanks to Nigel Clark for this formation of thought.

of the Anthropocene makes scientists arbiters, to an extent, of the human–environment relationship, itself an act with consequences beyond geology.

While there is recognition from geologists of the power of naming in the formalization of the Anthropocene—"formalization is a complex question because, unlike with prior subdivisions of geological time, the potential utility of a formal Anthropocene reaches well beyond the geological community" (Waters et al. 2016, 137)—this awareness of the social stakes is accompanied by a claim of the neutrality of geology as a "pragmatic" and "dispassionate" practice. Waters et al. say,

> We are aware of the narratives that may be built around the Anthropocene, and how these may be influenced by boundary choice. However, we suggest that the positioning of a stratigraphic boundary should simply be pragmatically and dispassionately chosen, by the same manner in which all earlier stratigraphic boundaries were chosen, to allow the most effective practical division between what would then become (by definition) Anthropocene and pre-Anthropocene strata and history. Such a choice would, we consider, be the best guarantee that wider discussion is solidly founded on the best factual basis available. (137)

What is considered as a dimension of the possible scope of this new political geology (part geoscience, part planetary alarm) is quickly acknowledged and then passed over as geology is consigned back to inhuman objecthood and objective language. Geology as a mode of embodied thinking remains restricted, unable to acknowledge the excess of this praxis in either world or subject-making dimensions.

1610

The earliest suggested date in the history of material exchanges is the 1610 thesis (Lewis and Maslin 2015), dating the Anthropocene's start to the European invasion of the Americas, or "New World," and the so-called exchange in flora and fauna. Authors Simon

Lewis and Mark Maslin call this the "Collision of the Old and New Worlds." Tying the Anthropocene to conquest makes explicit the colonial relation, but how does this rupture of bodies, flesh, and worlds become buried in the notion of exchange and contact? On his second voyage in 1493 to the New World (modern Dominica), Columbus initiates the first transatlantic slave voyage, a shipment of several hundred Taino people sent from Hispaniola to Spain. In 1496, he returns from his second voyage, carrying around thirty Native American slaves. By 1510, there is the start of the systematic transportation of African slaves to the New World. By the time Shakespeare's play *The Tempest* is first performed in 1611 (a year after the proposed start date), the enslaved figures of Caliban and Ariel are familiar subjects in the Old World. The "collision of the Old and New" covers over the friction of a less smooth, more corporeal set of racialized violences. In the language of exchange, it might be assumed that something was given rather than just taken. In that slippage of grammar, I want to shake the innocence of a language of description that assails this dehumanizing logic and masks its operations. The "nonevent" of this geologic corporeality is the very contact zone of geosocial relations that the Anthropocene attempts to speak to, yet it continues to do so in the progressive narrative arc, which is also a narrative of the asymmetries of colonial possession (of subjects, land, resources) and indigenous and black dispossession. This "exchange" is the directed colonial violence of forced eviction from land, enslavement on plantations, in rubber factories and mines, and the indirect violence of pathogens through forced contact and rape. Invasion instigates the disruption of ecological belonging and viable food economies and the introduction of famine and permanent malnutrition. It is the mutilation of land, personhood, spirituality, sexuality, and creativity. "No human contact, but relations of domination and submission" (Césaire [1972] 2000, 42). It was a process of alienation from geography, self, and the possibility of relation. Yet, "these heads of men, these collections of ears [collected by the barrelful by Count d'Hérisson], these burned houses, these Gothic invasions, this streaming blood, these cities that evaporate at the edge of the sword, are not to be so easily disposed of" (41). Césaire argues that the deliberate destruction and pride in dehumanization that characterized colonial conquest was not just a butchery that was inflicted on the colonized but one that also brutalized the colonizer: "the West has never been further from being able to live a true humanism—a humanism made to the measure of the world" (73). The superimposition of colonialism was a shearing of subjects from geography and the reinstantiation of those subjects into a category of geology that recoded them as property, whereby extraordinary possibilities in relation to the earth were wiped out.

The arrival of Europeans in the Caribbean in 1492 and the subsequent colonialism of the Americas "led to the largest human population replacement in the past 13,000 years" and to the mixing of previous separate biotas, such as corn, maize, potatoes, sugarcane, wheat, and domesticated animals such as cows, rats, goats, and pigs in new ecological formations and plantation ecologies of the Americas (Lewis and Maslin 2015).[2] As Europeans invaded the Caribbean, deforming and decimating the indigenous "Caribs," they began to use the islands as an experimental archipelago in terms of both the social organization of categories of human *and* the ecological arrangements of flora and fauna. The invasion of Europeans in the Americas resulted in a massive genocide of the indigenous population, leading to a decline from 54 million people in the Americas in 1492 to approximately 6 million in 1650, a result of murder, enslavement, famine, and disease. This led to a massive reduction in farming and the regeneration of forests and carbon uptake or sequestration by forests, leading to an observed decline in Antarctic ice cores of CO_2 in the atmosphere. This "Orbis spike" of systematic murder marks the instigation of Global-World-Space (an understanding of the world as a global entity that is

2. http://www.nhm.ac.uk/nature-online/life/plants-fungi/seeds -oftrade/page.dsml?section=crops&page=spread&ref=maize.

open to the conquest of the entirety of its spatialized and subjective relations). Here the enslaved are coded in parallel with material extraction under the guise of exchange. "Colonization = thingification" (Césaire [1972] 2000, 42), where subjectivity becomes fungible as a geographical as well as psychic and property entity. As a descriptive project in the grammar of geology, this spike naturalizes European colonial relations and their epistemological and ecological transformations. The Anthropocene cannot dust itself clean from the inventory of which it was made: from the cut hands that bled the rubber, the slave children sold by weight of flesh, the sharp blades of sugar, all the lingering dislocation from geography, dusting through diasporic generations. The shift of grammar cannot keep the rawness out.

The 1610 natal moment does, however, tie the origin of the Anthropocene to the death of 50 million indigenous people (80 to 95 percent of the population), systematic violence, and chattel slavery. This spike of brutality, sadism, and death, coupled with the subsequent dispossession of indigenous peoples from their land and the beginnings of industrial global slavery, enacts a foundational spatial inscription of colonialism (and race) into a monument of global environmental change. Inscribed in this origin of the Anthropocene is what Michael Taussig (1986, 4) calls a "space of death." The Anthropocene began with the annihilation of the Colonial Other and an epochal redescription of geography as Global-World-Space (Yusoff 2017a). That is, the fungibility of Blackness and geologic resources (as land, minerals, and ores) is coeval, predicated on the ability of the colonizer to both describe and operationalize world-space as a global entity (see Silva 2007). In this spike, the colonial Other is displaced, along with existing ecological relations and connections of the colonized to earth. As Global-World-Space is established by the colonizers, the Human and its Others are bifurcated in the production of racial difference to create two worlds of colonizer and colonized—or two different species, as Fanon would have. Coloniality cuts across both flesh and earth in the economies of valuation it established, exacting an "incorporative exclusion from space" (Moten 2016, 12) for the colonized as subjective agents and agents of geography. Indigenous genocide and removal from land and enslavement are prerequisites for power becoming operationalized in premodernity, a way in which subjects get (what Wynter names) "selected" or "dysselected" from geography and coded into colonial possession through dispossession.

The color line of the colonized was not merely a consequence of these structures of colonial power or a marginal effect of those structures; it was/is a means to operationalize extraction (therefore race should be considered as foundational rather than as periphery to the production of those structures and of global space). Richard Eden, in the popular 1555 publication *Decades of the New World,* compares the people of the "New World" to a blank piece of "white paper" on which you can "paynte and wryte" whatever you wish. "The Preface to the Reader" describes the people of these lands as inanimate objects, blank slates waiting to be civilized by the Europeans:

> these simple gentiles lyvinge only after the lawe of nature, may well bee likened to a smoothe and bare table unpainted, or a white paper unwritten upon, upon the which yow may at the first paynte and wryte what yow lyste. (sig. C3v)

As land is made into tabula rasa for European inscription of its militant maps, so too do Indigenes and Africans become rendered as a writ or ledger of flesh scribed in colonial grammars.

"Black Metamorphosis," 1452

Wynter suggests that we should in fact consider 1452 as the beginning of the New World, as African slaves are put to work on the first plantations on the Portuguese island of Madeira, initiating the "sugar–slave" complex—a massive replantation of ecologies and forced relocation of people (existing ecologies were not immune to the ravages of the new invaders, from plants and domestic animals to microbiomes and new geomorphic regimes). Wynter argues that the importance of the New World is in its dual processes of the "reduction of Man to Labour and of Nature to Land under the impulsion of the market economy." Wynter forcefully demonstrates how "Man" appears as the ontological signification of Whiteness and how this rational man is established as the biologically selected being, established first through Cartesian man and then through biologism as an advanced evolutionary subject within concepts of geologic time. Weheliye (2002, 27) calls this "dis-dentification, wherein whiteness connotes the full humanity only gleaned in relation to the lack of humanity in blackness." The effect of this doubling of Man/Whiteness in the natal moment of "his" heuristic formation disabuses the idea of humanity as an ontological category that has a nonracialized primacy. Weheliye argues, "In black culture this category becomes a designation that shows its finitudes and exclusions very clearly, thereby denaturalizing the 'human' as a universal formation while at the same time laying claim to it" (27). In reclaiming humanity as a heuristic operation rather than an ontological formation, Wynter plots the historic formation of Man as a racialized subject that is exclusionary at the point of origin, and precisely because of the history of those murderous origins. Wynter adds to her revolutionary formation of Man[3] (and his overrepresentation) in "Black Metamorphosis," where she considers the relations between land and territory in

---

3. Wynter (2015, 23) reminds us that the "larger issue is, then, the incorporation of all forms of human being into a single homogenized descriptive statement that is based on the figure of the West's liberal monohumanist *Man*. And this conception of being, because ostensibly natural-scientific, is biocentric." Thus this *Man* is restricted in its biopolitical horizon to a liberal form of subjectivity that denies the ecologies and geophysics of existence. Furthermore, as Katherine McKittrick argues, "the human is tied to epistemological histories that presently value a genre of the human that reifies Western bourgeois tenets; the human is therefore wrought with physiological and narrative matters that systematically excise the world's most marginalized" (quoted in Wynter 2015, 9).

the organization of Colonial Man's "humanity" and the geographies of erasure that underpin it in this conquest of space.

Wynter argues that the invention of the figure of Man in 1492 as the Portuguese travel to the Americas instigates at the same time "a *refiguring* of humanness" (Silva 2015, 93) in the idea of race. This refiguring of slaves trafficked to gold mines is borne into the language of the inhuman, whereupon Blackness becomes characterized through its ledger of matter, which in turn populates the idea of race. Extending Wynter's argument, 1492 marks also the structural inclusion of Man's Others into the geological lexicon of the inhuman (as matter and energy) and the exclusion from its material wealth, whereby humanness becomes differentiated by the inhuman objectification of indigenous and black subjects. While Wynter argues that this devaluation of Blackness served the specific material purpose of labor and the colonization of Indian land, there is also a prior step in the identification of inhuman objects that generated the context of "needs" for such labor and dispossession. Voiding subjects was also about voiding a relation to earth that was embodied, organized, and intensified by those relations to place; taking place is also taking ways in which people realize themselves through the specific geologies of a land. Colonialism enacted multiple forms of geologic disruption as well as the more obvious forms of extractive dispossessions.

Wynter contends that the revaluation of black life and the resistance to dehumanization could only be made through the "creation of a counter-culture through the transplantation of their old cultures onto a strange soil, its reinvention in new and alien conditions. It was in this transplantation, this metamorphosis of an old culture into a new, that the blacks made themselves indigenous to their new land" (Wynter n.d., 46–47). This also involved the

transplantation of a traditional relationship to nature, a relationship under the inspiration of which the slave, now in exile, both adapted himself to Nature and transformed it. In this type of relationship the *land* (i.e. part of Nature) could not be regarded as a mere commodity in the land-labor-capital-relationship. New world land, like the land in Africa was still seen as the Earth—the communal means of production. This attitude, transferred and perpetuated, was the central grid for many old beliefs which could be retranslated into a new reality. (47)

Descriptions of the lives of slaves in Jamaica in the seventeenth century by English clergyman the Rev. John Taylor stress the "great veneration" which the slaves had for "the Earth." It may be precisely because land and labor were regarded as private property that the earth became a source of possibility to release the literal stranglehold of that incarceration in a propertied relation.

In the struggle against forms of propertied relation with the inhuman, different intimacies developed with the earth. Wynter (n.d.) discusses the importance of the plot accorded to slaves to grow their own food in slave replantation. She says,

> The plot was the slave's area of escape from the plantation, it was an area of experience which reinvented and therefore perpetuated an alternative world view, alternative consciousness to that of the plantation. This world view was *marginalized* by the plantation but never destroyed. In relation to the plot, the slave lived in a society partly created as an adjunct to the market, partly as an end in itself. (53)

While growing food was a basic requirement for the reproduction of labor power for the plantation, it also became part of the reproduction of cultural powers in a new land, to establish a less alienated relation to the earth: "Let me be contained between latitude and longitude" (Césaire [1956] 1969, 28). The relation of slave to provision ground was a relation to a contingent earth, a material relation forged in resistance to the dehumanizing of colonialism that opened a carceral geography.

The earth in its symbolic and nonabstracted forms (as a knowledge about survival in maroonage, the quotidian practices of harvesting useful plants and animals, and navigation) was a crucial aspect of slave revolts. Wynter (n.d., 71) argues, "Black slavery in the Caribbean was synonymous with black revolt against slavery. And these revolts would be crucial to the indigenization process." Maroonage becomes the practice of cultural resistance to slavery. Wild mountain and interior living was also a successful part, Wynter argues, of replantation to the new land and the confrontation with its unfamiliar geographical conditions. She discusses at length the oaths to earth that were sworn before rebellions and how these were oaths to ancestors replanted in a new land—and that such oaths could not be broken despite the horrendous torture of those captured, in a context where "property that had rebelled, thereby affirming its status as human, must be burnt (i.e. tortured) as a 'terror' to other 'property' who might want to assert their human status" (79). Kissing the earth before rebellions was an oath-act that maintained a social contract with the earth often to the point of death (81–83). Wynter argues that this "indigenization"[4] was a way of thinking and apprehending the material reality of slavery through a dynamic replanting of roots (or "transplanting" as Wynter calls it) in an alien context: "this is the process of black cultural resistance and response to the Middle Passage and to what lay on the farther side—the alienated reality of a New World, new not only in its geography, but also in its radically different experience" (7). Disrupting the grammar of the inhuman articulated through thirteenth- to nineteenth-century genealogies of race, planting roots through maroonage and cultivation established kinship with the earth, made in the context of natal alienation.

In the path of the totality of alienation, the achievement in Haiti was to put down roots in a "stranger" soil, which "made the soil their own" (Wynter, n.d., 17) in ways that were not predicated on

---

4. Wynter's claim on indigenization and learning new forms of planting subjectivity in the earth is a means to claim back a stolen subjective-geographic relation and should not be confused with a claim of indigeneity. Within the context of settler colonialism, indigeneity rightly makes specific material claims about sovereignty and territory that are different from the claims that Wynter is making for black slaves. I believe Wynter is arguing for us to notice the creation of new material grammar outside of plantation geo-logics that humanize inhuman conditions through a relation to the earth that is planetary, not territorial.

the notion of territory under colonialism. As Price-Mars (quoted in Wynter, n.d.) said, the planet rather than humanism became the sphere of recognition for the Haiti Revolution; "our presence on a spot of that American archipelago which we 'humanized,' the breach which we made in the process of historical events to snatch our place among men," was worthy of study, a particular achievement that could be placed "within the common life of man on the planet" (Wynter, n.d., 17). Such a rupture in the fabric of colonialism's codification of personhood and space was an extraordinary reclamation of both freedom and its geographical expression. Wynter argues that since "needs produce powers just as powers produce needs," the response to the dehumanizing alienation was "to *create* the new vocabulary of the new existence" (Price-Mars, as quoted in Wynter, n.d., 18). Wynter argues that alienation is an inherently dynamic concept that implies change, "a consciousness of being alienated." For Price-Mars, the study of the folklore of Haiti was a study of transplantation, where indigeneity becomes fused with the site of the struggle, essentially a geographical, soil-based process of rerooting and of learning new forms of planting oneself in the earth. "Haiti where negritude rose to its feet for the first time and said it believed in its own humanity" (Césaire [1956] 1969, 29). Wynter (n.d.) calls this process "cultural metamorphosis," but it is also a geological metamorphosis tethered to the place, site, and soil of struggle.

While slave owners tried to void their subjects as inhuman objects, Wynter (n.d.) argues that black culture was creative because it had to overcome its property status to find other means of revaluation. As slaves were traded as both property and standard equivalence (for a certain amount of gold ounces), as "Native trade goods—gold, slaves, pepper, ivory, native cloths, hides, cattle and millet—were used as standards. Some European stables such as iron bars, coppers and cloth were used," the slave became interned in "metamorphosis from human entity to a market one" (32–33). Revaluation, then, required a destabilization of the relations of production in the realm of aesthetics and sense:

in other words, the oath-taking ceremonies and subsequent revolts were at one and the same time a form of praxis and an abstract theoretical activity. Neither could be separated from the other. The theory only existed in praxis; praxis was inseparable from theory. (Wynter, n.d., 139)

The embodied experience of power located in the earth was the basis of knowledge and the affirmation of a more exorbitant world or planetarity. The articulation of resistance is not a romantic appeal but a structural reorientation to the rifts of colonialism and its geosocial formations, made through the interarticulation of the inhuman in the breaks of propertied forms (see Davies 2015). This revaluation or reconstruction of value deuniversalizes the effect of the language of the inhuman. In the savage New World, the exchange was of terror, slavery, and subjugation, of barbarous executions, disfigurement, and sadistic pleasures. That is, there was no exchange; there was replantation and resistance in the praxis of the human through a relation with the earth.

1800

The natal moment of the 1800 Industrial Revolution, first suggested by Crutzen (2002) and favored by social scientists, locates Anthropocene origination in capitalist modes of economic and ecological production, specifically its labor forms and technological innovations. This is the tale of entrepreneurship of a few white men transforming the world with their ingenuous creations or of a political economy that is aggressively sutured to the earth's processes via the lifeblood of fossil fuels. So the explorer as hero (Columbus) is replaced by the inventor as hero (Watt and his engine) in the progress narrative of Man as the agentic center and authority of power, cut with some European genius myth to rarefying the white male subject and his imperial intellectualism. Unsurprisingly, the Capitalocene, as it was quickly redubbed, became the site of numerous investigations into the "new" metabolisms of technology and matter enabled by the combination of fossil fuels, new engines, and the world as market. It relocated the Anthropocene back to Europe, to Britain, and claimed the history of the planet from this origination point. The revolutionary character of industrialization, as a transformative one-way street in the production of the commodity form and rising concentrations of CO_2 in the atmosphere, solidified in narratives as the new "sire" of geologic force. What the proliferation of Anthropocene discourse around industrialization, which I am not going to address in any detail here, does indicate is that the Anthropocene is not reducible to anthropogenic climate change or to a carbon or capitalist imaginary (or capitalism as a carbon imaginary). As Povinelli (2016) warns us, the carbon imaginary sutures us to a very particular rendering of life and death in late liberalism, one based on the governance of life through splicing the difference between geological and biological existence (see also Yusoff 2018). The racialization of epistemologies of life and nonlife is important to note here, particularly how this biocentrism (as per Wynter) prioritizes a white biopolitics. As Povinelli argues, carbon imaginaries are a site of social reproduction in the politics of knowledge—a politics that actively constructs indigenous peoples on the outside of its paradigmatic purview.

While capitalist commodity forms and their propertied relations undoubtedly transformed the atmosphere with the production of greenhouse gases (GHGs) through the burning vast quantities of coal, the creation of another kind of weather had already established its salient forms in the mine and on the plantation. Paying attention to the prehistory of capital and *its* bodily labor, both within coal cultures and on plantations that literally put "sugar in the bowl" (as Nina Simone sings), in those laboring workers forging the material conversions of the revolution, the muscular energy of slavery and capitalism become conglomerated. The new modes of material accumulation and production in the Industrial Revolution are relational to and dependent on their *pre*productive forms in slavery and its organization of human property as extractable energy properties. Wynter argues that the racism inherent in the construction of Europe was a complex part of the apparatus by which Western capitalism (and, ipso facto, Western civilization) fulfilled it extractive imperative and that global capitalism cannot be understood apart from large-scale black slavery out of Africa. Rather than slavery predating capitalist forms of labor, Wynter (n.d., 106) argues that the interrelation of slave labor power and free labor power in sugar production meant that the

> plantation was an intrinsic and functional part of a capitalist system which consisted of a mode of production based on free wage labor coexisting and dependent on a mode of production based on slave labor. . . . The plantation mode of production was not, therefore, an anomaly within the capitalist system, it was intrinsic to the system.

As C. L. R. James ([1938] 1989) argues in *Black Jacobins,* the immense wealth from the slave trade and the Haitian sugar plantations enriched the bourgeoisies to such an extent that they were powerful enough to set in motion the French Revolution:

> In other words both the hegemony of the Western bourgeoisie and of capitalism were in their origin based mainly on New World land, the forced labor of the Indian, and the conversion of man—the black man—into a commodity. The latter large-scale de-humanization of the European proletariat, *followed* on and *did not precede* the total negation of the black as human. Capitalism as a system therefore required the negation of the black as human. Far from being an anomaly in the rational: system of capitalism, black slavery was rationally central to capitalism as a system. (Wynter, n.d., 45–46, emphasis original)

At a material level, Catherine Hall's project *Legacies of British Slave-Ownership* makes visible the complicity in terms of structures of slavery and industrialization that organized in advance the categories of dispossession that are already in play and historically constitute the terms of racialized encounter of the Anthropocene. In 1833, Parliament finally abolished slavery in the British Caribbean, and the taxpayer payout of £20 million in "compensation" built the material, geophysical (railways, mines, factories), and imperial infrastructures of Britain and its colonial enterprises and empire. As the project empirically demonstrates, these legacies of colonial slavery continue to shape contemporary Britain. A significant proportion of funds were invested in the railway system connecting London and Birmingham (home of cotton production and gun manufacturing for plantations), Cambridge and Oxford, and Wales and the Midlands (for coal). Insurance companies flourished and investments were made in the Great Western Cotton Company, for example, and in cotton brokers, as well as in big colonial land companies in Canada (Canada Land Company) and Australia (Van Diemen's Land Company) and a number of colonial brokers. Investments were made in the development of metal and mineralogical technologies: Tyne Iron Co. Iron Works; Llynvi Iron Works; Dalnotter Iron Co.; New Shotts Iron Co.; Ynyscedwyn Iron Co.; J. J. Cordes; the Smithfield Company; Bristol Brass Wire and Copper Co.; Pendleton Colliery; Thomas Whitby & Co. coal, iron, and marble company; Castles and Rudgeway coal company; Arigna Iron and Coal Mining Co.; Company for the Working of Mines, Minerals and Metals; Port Philip and Colonial Gold Mining Co.; Potosi La Paz and Peruvian Mining Association; Annotto Bay Mining Association; Alpujarras Lead Co.; and Trinidad Petroleum Co. Other funds were reinvested into Plantations Caribbean, sugar brokers and refiners, tobacco brokers, West Indian merchants, and Dominica merchants. As a ledger, the financial benefits of ending slavery reshaped the world to provide the material *pre*conditions for the Industrial Revolution and the metamorphosis of capitalist forms. As the *Legacies* project evidences and Silva (2014, 2) argues, if we pay attention to the refiguring of the commodity in the consideration of colonial expropriation, "against the conventional view that places slavery in the prehistory of capital," a case can be made in this instance for how the total value produced by slave labor continues to sustain global capital through accumulation and legacy. In this ledger of investment and the materialization of industrialization and empire sits an unseen, unrecorded history withdrawn from view in the syntax of slavery that foreshadows and reinscribes across all these relations of the globalization of capital.

The slave–sugar–coal nexus both substantially enriched Britain and made it possible for it to transition into a colonial industrialized power (triggering a massive spike in Britain's population that maps directly onto its sugar and coal production). As Marx ([1867] 1961, 760) caustically observed, "the discovery of gold and silver in America, the extirpation, enslavement and entombment in mines of the aboriginal population . . . the turning of Africa into a warren for the commercial hunting of black-skins, signalled the rosy dawn of the era of capitalist production." The slave trade, he argued, was part of the primitive accumulation of capital that preceded and fashioned the economic conditions (and institutions, such as the insurance and finance industries) for industrialization. Slavery and industrialization were tied by the various afterlives of slavery in the form of indentured and carceral labor that continued to enrich new emergent industrial powers from both the Caribbean plantations and the antebellum South. Enslaved "free" African Americans predominately mined coal in the corporate use of black power or the new "industrial slavery," as Blackman (2008) terms it. The Alabama Iron Ore and Tennessee Coal and Iron companies were the largest convict labor companies and fed the coal mines of the U.S. Steel Corporation, which built the country. Blackman argues that most enslaved mine labor in the United States occurred after the abolition of slavery in 1865 and primarily fed the industrialization of America. The labor of the coffel—the carceral penance of the rock pile, "breaking rocks out here and keeping on the chain gang" (Nina Simone, *Work Song,* 1966), laying iron on the railroads—is the carceral future mobilized at plantation's end (or the "nonevent" of emancipation). As Marx ([1867] 1961, 759–60) puts it, "the veiled slavery of the wage-workers in Europe needed, for its pedestal, slavery pure and simple in the new world. . . . Capital comes dripping from head to foot, from every pore, with blood and dirt." Arguably, the racial circumscription of slavery predates and prepares the material ground for Europe and the Americas in terms of both nation *and* empire building—and continues to sustain it.

1950s

While the biostratigraphic signal from colonizing the Americas remains incompletely documented according to the AWG, the favored stratigraphic marker by many authors, owing to its widespread and globally synchronous signal, is the nuclear radioisotope's from the fallout from weapons testing. According to the AWG, the geochemical residue from the Trinity atomic device at Alamogordo, New Mexico, detonated on July 16, 1945, is the start of the Global Standard Stratigraphic Age (Zalasiewicz et al. 2015). Plutonium (^{239,240}Pu) is suggested as a good trace due to its ability to absorb into clays and organic compounds within marine sediments and because of its mostly artificial radionuclide suite, with a half-life of 24,110 years, that will be detectable in sedimentary deposits for some 100,000 years into the future (Waters et al. 2016). But as Elizabeth DeLoughrey (2013, 179) reminds us, it is not just the environment that bears the trace of these "tests"; "the body of every human on the planet now contains strontium90, a man-made by-product of nuclear detonations and forensic scientists use the traces of militarized radioactive carbon in our teeth to date human remains (as before or after the 1954 *Bravo* shot)." The nuclear stratigraphic trace would mark the more geologically dispersed events of the "Great Acceleration" of the 1950s, with its material conversions of fossil fuels; dissemination of black carbon, inorganic and spherical carbonaceous particles, worldwide; new geochemical compounds of polyaromatic hydrocarbons, polychlorinated biphenyls, and pesticide residues; doubling of soil nitrogen and phosphorus due to the Haber Bosch process of artificially producing nitrogen fertilizer; and dispersals of new materials, such as aluminum, concrete, plastics, and synthetic fibers. This array of material transformations and new mineral evolutions has both transformed the balance of geochemical materials on the earth's surface and introduced new geological substances and forces into the planetary mix.

Japanese artist Isao Hashimoto's *2053*[5] records a time-lapse map in a series of blips and flashes of the nuclear explosions that have taken place between 1945 and 1998, signaling that the test does not hold exclusive rights to any one domain; it overflows, accumulates, and seemingly disappears, all the while reorganizing exposures. These blips and flashes do, however, have a black and indigenous intensification. Nuclear testing marks the displacement and exposure of indigenous peoples in the Pacific Islands and the radiation of Native American and Aboriginal peoples in North America and Australia. Many islanders in the Pacific were moved and removed during U.S. nuclear tests. Bikini Atoll, for example, was subjected to thirty years of nuclear explosions, during which time islanders were moved to a range of islands (to Rongerik, then to Kwajalein). Islanders in the Atolls were both proximate to the nuclear fallout, where they were exposed to radioactive ash, and moved to uninhabitable islands, where islanders "sucked stones" to keep hunger at bay and starvation was common. Many returned to Bikini Island, despite the contamination of its water sources and foodstuffs, because the uninhabited islands to which they were moved were uninhabited for a reason. Islanders on Rongelap and Utrok exposed by the Bravo detonation (six islands were vaporized and fourteen left uninhabitable) were subject to immediate radiation from the blasts and suffered visible burns, causing both immediate and lasting epidemiological legacies and toxic intimacies with leukemia, neoplasms, and thyroid cancers. The white powder of irradiated coral dust that fell throughout the Atolls was dangerously radioactive. Not recognizing this new material substance, children played in it. As Maori poet Hone Tuwhare's 1964 poem goes, this was "No Ordinary Sun." The fallout coated Marshallese bodies, ground, trees, bread fruit, coconuts, crabs, fish, and water. This nuclear colonialism fused thermonuclear sand and poisoned air, water,

5. https://www.youtube.com/watch?v=LLCF7vPanrY.

and soil, dispersing radioactive elements of strontium, cesium, and iodine across strata and into bone in brown bodies.

After Bravo, the U.S. military waited seventy-two hours to pick up those exposed and transport them to Kwajalein Atoll (the location of the U.S. base) for medical examination. The 236 Marshallese were stripped naked and sprayed down before boarding the vessel. At the army base, they were treated as test subjects for the effects of radiation. The Bravo detonation instigated the human experiments in Project 4.1,[6] a secret U.S. Atomic Energy Commission (AEC) study, which was planned for and then authorized while Marshallese were being treated on Kwajalein and continued for years to monitor the effects of radiation on a human population. Marshallese were subjected to unconsented medical testing, and a "cross section of happy, amenable savages" (as the scientist in the AEC promotional film informs us) were brought to Chicago for examination as specimens for experimentation in a human zoo dressed up in suits "that they had to return to the U.S. government in Hawaii."[7] Spillers (2003, 208) suggests (on the practice of medical experimentation on sick Negroes and the profitable "atomizing" of diseased body parts) that "the procedures adopted for the captive flesh demarcate a total objectification, as the entire captive community becomes a living laboratory." Women gave birth to what they called "jellyfish babies" because of their translucent skin and soft or absent bones. There were many congenital disorders and miscarriages. "Marshallese cancers" were some of the highest recorded in the world. The AEC film *Operation Castle* nar-

6. 'Project 4.1 Biomedical Studies: Studies of Response of Human Beings Exposed to Significant Beta and Gamma Radiation due to Fall-Out from High Yield Weapons": "The purposes of [Project 4.1] were to (1) evaluate the severity of radiation injury to the human beings exposed, (2) provide for all necessary medical care, and (3) conduct a scientific study of radiation injuries to human beings" (Martin and Rowland 1982, 186, 188).

7. The use and return of the suits indicate a certain performative quality in the U.S. military's subjection of the Marshallese citizens, not unlike the rented clothing that slave dealers used on the slave blocks.

rates, "These islands, functioning as *s,* gave us our first real clues to the vast area affected by contamination from a high yield surface burst" (quoted in DeLoughrey 2013, 171). Islanders were returned when it was known that the island was heavily contaminated to study them as fallout "collectors" of nuclear bombs. As Spillers (2003, 207) elucidates, the grammar of containment in Blackness was a category mobilized to obscure and subjugate the human in these human experiments:

> The anatomical specifications of rupture, of altered human tissue, take on the objective description of laboratory prose. . . . These undecipherable markings on the captive body render a kind of hieroglyphics of the flesh whose severe disjunctures come to be hidden to the cultural seeing by skin color.

This nuclear colonialism in the Pacific and Marshall islands used a brown strata of bodies to mitigate and absorb its geochemical shocks.

The geographies of colonial territories were key sites and subjects for the performance of militarization and scientific development (but there is no such thing as a nuclear "test"). As DeLoughrey (2013, 172) argues,

> Western colonizers had long configured tropical islands into the contained spaces of a laboratory, which is to say a suppression of island history and indigenous presence. This generation of AEC ecologists embraced nuclear testing as creating a novel opportunity to study a complete ecosystem through the trace of radiation. . . . An American empire of tropical islands, circling the globe from the Pacific to the Caribbean, became a strategic space for military experimentation and the production of new scientific epistemologies like ecosystem theory.

For example, Britain exploded seven nuclear tests and seven hundred subtests[8] on the Aboriginal land of Maralinga Tjaruta in

8. The subtests involving plutonium, uranium, and beryllium and were code-named "Kittens," "Rats," and "Vixen," which ironically are representative of the feral ecologies that accompanied settlers and had such a devastating effect on the unique flora and fauna of Australia.

southern Australia, home of the Pitjantjara and Yankunytjatjara peoples, in 1956 and 1963. Many were forcibly resettled at Yalata, but attempts to curtail access to the Maralinga site were often unsuccessful due to strong ties to country, leading to exposure to nuclear contamination. The first French test, Gerboise Bleue, was conducted in February 1960, in the context of the Algerian War (1954–62). From 1960 to 1996, France carried out 210 nuclear tests, 17 in the Algerian Sahara and 193 in French Polynesia in the South Pacific, causing vast swaths radioactive fallout across Polynesia. In the Anthropocene backloop, these very islands in Polynesia and the Marshall Islands are now subjected to rising sea levels from climate change. The Anthropocene fossil of the waste repository in the Marshall Islands, the nuclear, forty-six-centimeter-thick "Runit" dome of Portland cement that covers the radioactive material from Bikini and other islands (there were forty-two tests in total on Enewetak Atoll alone from 1948), is leaching radioactive material, causing radionuclide migration into the marine environment. Rising sea levels and the intensification of storm events threaten to take the islands and their nuclear-fused strata into the sea.

The nuclear marker both commemorates a certain period of militarization and its global dissemination and distances the impacts and responsibility for those acts, tethering them to the Cold War and its "past" geopolitical concerns. The dialogic relation of this Golden Spike to the politics of the event is truncated, as it is lodged in the event of the atomic bomb and its technological achievements rather than the effects on the peoples and ecologies of the Pacific and the more widespread nuclear colonialism and its ongoing presents in nuclear waste. Canada and Australia, for example, as settler-colonial states, are the biggest extraterritorial mining countries and are involved in the disposal and location of nuclear waste on indigenous land, often in conflict with native title claims and predating on economic impoverishment. The disposal of wastes mobilizes a new frontierism in the designation of sacrifice zones within and beyond national borders that aggregates environmental harms with anti-Blackness.

Earth Archives, Geologic Subjects, and the Race of Strata

The continued siting or marking of indigenous territories and intergenerational flesh of indigenous populations through the exposures of environmental wastes—what is called environmental racism—prompts a need to extend Achille Mbembe's "Decolonizing Knowledge and the Question of the Archive"[9] to explore the role of earth archives as material deposits that maintain a colonial relation through the extractive and waste industries, particularly through the cojoined violences of extraction practices and their ongoing legacies of toxicity (see Bebbington and Bury 2013). For example, in the New World silver mines of South America, where as much as 136,000 metric tons of silver were produced between 1500 and 1800 (80 percent of global production), enslaved Africans (estimated to be about 4 million) were put work in the mines, replacing indigenous slaves because they were deemed to be better workers and more immune to diseases such as smallpox and typhus. Spanish slavery records show that Africans were considered essential in the operation of the mines and used them to extract enormous wealth, particularly from the mountain of Potosi (which received additional investment after the British 1833 slavery payout), where the average "working" life of a miner was six to eight years (on Southern sugar plantations, it was eight to ten years). It is estimated as many as 8 million may have died from mining accidents, lung diseases caused by the mineral dust, and contamination by the mercury used in processing the silver. Nicholas Robbins (2011) argues that there was a double genocide: the initial invasion of the New World and its impact on indigenous people, then a second wave of genocide through silver mining and the afterlives of mercury pollution into the soil, ecologies, and bodies of local communities.

9. https://africaisacountry.atavist.com/decolonizing-knowledge-and -the-question-of-the-archive.

Similarly, the uranium mining for nuclear industry exploited and polluted Native American lands and bodies in the United States and returns in the nuclear colonialism of waste and superfund sites, where economic poverty is used as an exploitative means to reterritorialize land with the "by-products" of nuclear testing (see Kuletz 1998, 126–27). Contemporaneously, the effects of ecoimperialist measures such as REDD in the Amazon that evicted indigenous peoples of their land in attempts to offset carbon emission created elsewhere and the location of waste sites in low-income and predominately black neighborhoods continue this disproportionate legacy of harm. The imperative is to recognize the regime of offsetting—of carbon, ecosystems, deforestation, pollution, forced migration, land grabs, climate change—as a neocolonial enterprise that continues extraction through displacement of waste and the ongoing legacy of colonial "experiments." This offsetting is achieved through the grammar of materiality that privileges equivalents above relation. As poet Kathy Jetñil-Kijiner from the Marshall Islands says, "these two issues—they're so much bigger than us, nuclear issues and climate change and yet we [the Marshall Islands] are at that crossroad" (Laubscher 2017). In rejoinder, fellow Marshellese poet Terisa Tenei Siagatonu claims, "Everyone is effected [sic] by climate change but some are effected [sic] first. . . . For those of us who might not have the language but are still able to speak, for those of us that can't afford rent but can't afford to wait."[10] Placed at the axis of environmental impacts, the language of "dispassionate" geology betrays itself as an economy of displacement (subjective and environmental).

As the Anthropocene names a universal geology from below, it renders a violent homogenization of subjective affects and material possibilities. The move *toward* a more expansive notion of humanity must be made with care. It cannot be based on the pre-

10. Terisa Tinei Siagatonu, "Layers," http://themissingslate.com/2017/10/01/layers/.

supposition that emancipation is possible once the racial others and their voices are included finally to realize this universality but must be based on the recognition that these "Others" are already inscripted in the foundation formulation of the universal *as a space of privileged subjectification*. Through the categories of nonbeing, trajectories of colonial enterprise exclude the very subjects who make up the racialized strata of extraction and exposure. This flesh gets spiked by the Anthropocene. Thinking flesh with Spillers, as the conceptual expansion and excess of the contraction of a person into a thing, then, "we mean its seared, divided, ripped-apartness, riveted to the ship's hole, fallen, or 'escaped' over board" (Spillers 2003, 206) muscularity. The division between body and flesh is an essential category difference between a captive and liberated subject position. Flesh is the "zero degree of social conceptualization that does not escape concealment under the brush of discourse or the reflexes of iconography" (Spillers 2003, 206). The geologic claims on and in black and brown flesh establish stratigraphic traces that are both bone deep and intergenerational, marking bodies with nuclear radioisotopes and skin with codes of disposability in the proximity to power and toxicity.

Precisely because modernity (and premodernity) is secured in a subjectivity that is inscripted at the onset in race, the diagnostic of the Anthropocene does not unleash any ethical crisis in liberal discourse about who is targeted by these material practices. What is at stake and what is on the front line are defined through the color line. The disembodied monuments and matter of the Golden Spike point but don't name. This is why the Anthropocene is configured in a future tense rather than in recognition of the extinctions already undergone by black and indigenous peoples. Following in the wake of humanism, the production of the Anthropocene is predicated on Whiteness as the color of universality. While the ethical distinction of humanism rests on the distinction between what is human and what is inhuman, Blackness is established, as Mbembe argues, as the exception to this coda, consigned to the objecthood of inhuman matter. One major implication of Wynter's (2015, 23) thought is that "*humanness* is no longer a *noun. Being human is a praxis*" and cannot be taken for granted as a self-explanatory category or reason. And human as praxis intersects with geological classificatory practices to inform the category designations of what is inhuman. It is this very intimacy with the life of the inhuman that the tradition of critical black thought has engaged to resurrect the domains of life that seem to be in excess of this objective language, which transmutes black subjects into different categories of materiality. This is the unseen fragment of the Anthropocene archive that needs attention, as subject and relation. Silva (2007) argues that race is foundational rather than simply formative to the production of global subjectivity and space; race cannot be dismantled through acts of inclusion, because it is the building block in the modern world system and its anchor. Furthermore, the violence of grammars of geology must change to acknowledge this inscription and develop a mode of writing that speaks beyond the objecthood of geologic materiality to its inhuman and inhumane dimensions, as material praxis and subjective condition.

If we look at the suggested natal moments of the Anthropocene, the formative role of race in the genealogy of an Anthropocenic subject and the set of environmental processes that accrue in the new subjective mode of geologic force become apparent. This genealogy *from Colonial Man to Anthropocene Man* is evident in the constitution of Anthropocene scientific cultures and in the body of popular personifications of the Anthropocene. On the front cover of the scientific journal *Nature* (519, no. 7542 [2015]), the white male body of "Anthropocene Man" is pictured gently hemorrhaging biodiversity, with an atom cloud glowing a temperate warm orange on his shoulder. Ships crisscross the Middle Passage on his chest with the wind beneath their sails, like hipster tattoos, and little black bodies stand on Africa and the Americas, populating the corners of their triangular passage. The miniature blacks are only other bodies on display, inside the peeled back skin of white masculine modernity, posited alongside the equally sized cocoa, maize, and wheat. A cyborgian working of industry is revealed on his arm. The Human Epoch is blazed across his well-defined abs. Now read these images of Anthropocene Man next to Spillers's words: "That order [sociopolitical order of the New World], with its human sequence written in blood, *represents* for its African and indigenous peoples a scene of *actual* mutilation, dismemberment and exile. First of all, their New World, diasporic plight marked a *theft* of the *body*—a *willful* and violent (and unimaginable from this distance) severing of the captive body from its motive will, its active desire" (Spillers 2003, 206). Or take the cover of the *Smithsonian* magazine. What is represented is a Western scientist surveying the geologic bedrock, the lone liberal subject, individualized and in possession of the horizon that he surveys as his territorial acquisition. Such imagery, unsurprisingly, echoes with the colonial paintings that underpin this man's genealogy (such as the painting of Lewis and Clark's *Western Corps of Discovery* expedition 1804–6, *An Evening Reading* by Thomas Lorimer in 1941), where the cartographic imagination of the privileged surveyor accords both power and truth over the territory and a benign foresight that naturalizes the colonial gaze, reproducing and reinforcing this geopolitical conquest within a Western claim to globalism, with resonances of "Manifest Destiny." Rather than offering humanity as a cohesive possibility for Anthropocene politics, "the 'middle passages' of black culture to and in the New World are not marked so much by 'humanity' as by an acute lack thereof; a 'black hole' of humanity, so to speak" (Weheliye 2002, 26). Akin to Wright's idea of the Middle Passage to the New World as a "big bang of blackness," Ishamel Reed calls it "an Atlantic of blood. Repressed energy of anger that would form enough sun to light a solar system. A burnt-out black hole. A cosmic slave hole" (quoted in Weheliye 2002, 21). The passage to universalism in ecological or planetary terms without a redress of how that humanity was borne as an exclusionary construct, coterminus with the enslavement of some humans and the genocide of others, remains a questionable traverse.

However, contrasting (White) posthumanism and Afro-diasporic thinking, Weheliye (2002, 26) suggests that rather than dispensing with this category that was invented to hide its opposite (the inhuman), black scholars have sought to appropriate this category: "Afro-diasporic thinking has not evinced the same sort of distrust and/or outright rejection of 'man' in its universalist, post-Enlightenment guise as Western antihumanist or posthumanist philosophies. Instead, black humanist discourses emphasize the historicity and mutability of the 'human' itself, gesturing toward different, catachrestic, conceptualizations of this category." As King (2016, 1029) argues, "Blackness is raw dimensionality (symbol, matter, kinetic energy) used to make space. As space, Black bodies cannot also occupy space on human terms." Denied the space-time of the human, black people, King argues, must imagine place outside of humanist configurations of geography. While this other space-time of Blackness finds itself in the stars in Afro-futurism, there is considerable scope to find it in the quotidian spaces of the earth.

In the Anthropocenic reinscription of earth forces and global relations, Man is placed as a central organizing concept for planetary relations. This Man is both a figure of address and a mode of comprehension (if not a unit of analysis) that repositions the human in its liberal-humanist structural form at the axis of planetary concern. The "Age of Man" is a dominant and dominating mode of subjectification—of nature, the non-Western world, ecologies, and the planet. As in the illustration on the cover of *Nature*, Man is the body politic of global environmental change. This Man is heir apparent to the historical formations of Colonial Man and *the* privileged subject of biopolitical life. This ethical subject substantiates the hierarchies of subjectification while simultaneously maintaining the production of marginalities and minorities that fall outside of consideration in this secular yet universalizing mode. As Weheliye (2014, 8) suggests,

> since bare life and biopolitics discourse largely occludes race as a critical category of analysis, as do many other current articulations

of critical theory, it cannot provide the methodological instruments for diagnosing the tight bonds between humanity and racializing assemblages in the modern era. The volatile rapport between race and the human is defined above all by two constellations: first, there exists no portion of the modern human that is not subject to racialization, which determines the hierarchical ordering of Homo Sapiens species into humans, not-quite-humans, and nonhumans; second, as a result, humanity has held a very different status for the traditions of the radically oppressed. Man will only be abolished "like a face drawn in the sand at the edge of the sea" if we disarticulate the modern human (Man) from its twin: racializing assemblages.

The question Weheliye asks (after Wynter) in his book *Habeas Viscus* of these twins—the human and racializing assemblages—is, what different modalities of the human would come to light if the liberal-humanist figure of Man is not taken as the master-subject? Humanity continues to persist in its current forms of inhumanity precisely because it is a humanity that is racially constituted and where racial difference is produced as an oppositional form on the outside when it is really, as Silva argues through spatialized and subjective modes, internal to the formation of such humanity. This coterminous birth of Man and his Others forms the basis for the enlightenment subject of ethical consideration, the subject around which an understanding of humanity (and inhumanity) coheres (on the conatality of liberal notions of freedom in Hegel and the organization of slavery in Haiti, see Buck-Morss 2000). This birth codifies Whiteness with freedom and Blackness with objectification and slavery,[11] Blackness being the position of both the unfree and the *unthought* (Hartman and Wilderson 2003). And this is precisely why Whiteness (as a formation of power) gets to "choose" environmental conditions and black and brown are still the colors of environmental exhaustion and the exposures to excess.

Thinking, alongside Silva, toward a global idea of race that is

---

11. And even Otherness positioned in the pursuit of freedom was itself "romancing the shadow." Morrison (1992, 37–38) suggests, "The slave population, it could be and was assumed, offered itself up as surrogate selves

not at the margins of the conceptualization of the Western ethical subject but a crucial consideration of all its modes of spatial and subjective production would mean the abandonment of Colonial Man, alongside a shift in the forms and modes of expression outside of Western epistemic traditions. In the words of Angela Last, this would be to undo geopolitics through geopoetics (Last 2015, 2017). In Last's proposal, made through the work of Caribbean geopoetics, "decolonization utilizes the geophysical not as a model for human or human–world relations, but as a tool for re-situating oneself and for reimagining global divisions" (56). This matter relation that reterritorializes the inhuman as a geopoetic resource alerts us to the grammar of material divisions that organize subjective modes, wherein geopolitical agency is designated as a quality of a privileged biopolitical subject but also the potentials for a redescription of inhuman relations. As I have argued elsewhere, "it is the very division between 'dead matter' and the privileged 'live subject' that constitutes the active politics of recognition in late liberalism. This axial division of materiality into passive and active forms, that might or might not become subjects (depending on their status on the color line), is the current bite of geopolitics" (Yusoff 2018). A new language of the earth cannot be resolved in biopolitical modes (of inclusion) because of the hierarchical divisions that mark the biocentric subject.

Geologizing the Social

In the context of socializing geology and geologizing the social, the Anthropocene is but a blink in time in the deformation of the planet, but its original claim is to render a new quality of

---

for meditation on problems of human freedom, its lure and its exclusiveness. . . . Nature without limits, natal loneness, internal aggression . . . in other words, this slave population was understood to have offered itself up for reflections on human freedom in terms other than the abstractions of human potential and the rights of man.

the human. This origination and account of geologic mastery is another "category mistake" that can only be historically claimed if slavery and the rendering of subject as inhuman object is discounted from the experience of the human (thereby reinforcing its positioning outside the category of the human). The invasion of the "New World" produced the first geologic subjects of the Anthropocene, and they were indigenous and black. The inhuman, as both geologic property and mode of subjective relation in chattel slavery, rendered a coercive interpenetration between human and inhuman categories, or what Spillers calls an "alien intimacy" that predates the "new" imagined subject of the Anthropocene. Rather, diaspora was a social sedimentation that names the violence of geology in its inception, not as an overlooked aspect of spatial and environmental relation that can be subsequently claimed as mastery over nature and geologic force but as one that is more properly located in the grammar of *geologic determinism* established in genocide and the master–slave relation. This master–slave relation is initiated through the geologic praxis of extraction that required both slavery (first for mining) and its continuance as a mode of labor and psychic extraction of pleasure and sadism, which in turn codified Blackness in proximity to the qualities and properties of the inhuman. Defining an identity for an epoch through the geologizing of the social (and its modes of subjective relation), the origin stories of the Anthropocene construct a monolithic, post-racial "we" and singular temporality of being instead of differentiating geologic life along this praxis. Humanism is deployed as a method of erasure that obfuscates climate racism and social injustice in access to geography through differentiated histories of responsibilities and reward in geologic life (see Yusoff 2016, 6).

Wynter (2015, 24), discussing the formulation of the homogenized "we," suggests that this referent "is *not* the *referent-we* of the human species itself"; rather, it is isomorphic in its privileged subjectivity to the "we" of humanity. As Wynter goes on to suggest, as natural scientists and also bourgeois subjects, logically assume that the *referent-we*—whose normal behaviors are destroying the habitability of our planet—is that of *the human population as a whole.* The "we" who are destroying the planet in these findings are not understood as the *referent-we* of *homo oeconomicus* (a "we" that includes themselves/ourselves as bourgeois academics). *Therefore, the proposals that they're going to give for change are going to be devastating!* And most devastating of all for the global poor, who have already begun to pay the greatest price. . . . Devastating, because the proposals made, if nonconsciously so, are made from the perspective of *homo oeconomicus* and its attendant master discipline of economics. (24; emphasis original)

The assertion of this unity across time and space erases the very racialized ruptures and geosocial rifts that brought this Anthropocenic world into being through the stratification of flesh. As Toni Morrison (1992, 46) suggests, "the world does not become raceless or will not become unracialized by assertion. The act of enforcing racelessness in literary discourse is itself a racial act." The birth of racial subject is tied to colonialism and the conquest of space and the codification of geology as property and properties. Thereby geologic resources and bodily resources (or racialized slavery) share a natal moment.

Challenging the celebration of those histories that produce mythic accounts, underpinned by Western geologic modes of extraction and White Imperialism, is a way to challenge not just the narration of geology but *where* and *how* we might look for its marks in a decolonizing mode of geologic relation. Undoing what Hortense Spillers calls "grammars of capture" is a way to unearth how geology moves through Blackness rather than simply against it. That is to suggest that other material relations emerge through this deformation of subjective life. Originary moments, told as the event of geology, can be thought about as "interstitial—those punctualities (in a linked series of events) that go unmarked so that the mythic view remains undisturbed" (Spillers 2003, 14). In other words, origin stories bury as much as they reveal about material relations and their genealogies. And there is a need to *de*sediment the social life of geology, to place it in the terror of its coercive acts and the interstitial moments of its shadow geology—what I call a billion Black Anthropocenes.

Let's imagine for a moment, in the realm of a more exuberant and exacting social geology, that the Golden Spike is something that spikes or impales, that there is a flesh that underwrites this geology (human, nonhuman, inhuman). This corporeality is a way to visualize, to render sensible, to redress the social context and a contextual outside to that geology (where geology is never a formation only of materiality but also of time, and species and its twin race, explanation, and future politics). This contextual outside might be called the geotrauma of the Anthropocene's realization—a geotrauma where flesh is the medium of exchange that organizes and modifies the Spike. Geologic relations are always material relations of power, relations that are constituted through their passage, and it is a passage of resistance. Akin to the genre of colonial paintings in which the geographic surveyor plots a territory, those lines on a map and the collections of mineral artifacts they enable have consequences; they establish unfolding *geologics,* for particular bodies and subject positions, as disposable in the shadow economy of extraction.

Naming a Spike is not just scientific triumphalism but enacts and then describes a structure and emphasis of attention or monumentalization. These Golden Spikes are both cultural edifices of political geology and monuments to extractive–racialized–industrialized complexes. What these nominations are naming, albeit obscured in the narration, is a story about the very bodies that undo strata—the theft of bodies, of the flesh that hews the rock, that plants the sugar plantation, that blasts and gets blasted in the mines, that transports and carries the pathogens and pollutions of those Spikes *as* processes of destratifications. These subjective and material actualizations of the Anthropocene are geographies of violent coercion. There is an invisible agent that carries those Golden Spikes, in their flesh, chains, hunger, and bone, and in their social formations as sound, radical poetry, critical black studies, and subjective possibility realized against impossible conditions; there *are* a billion Black Anthropocenes that are its experiential witness and embody its modes of mattering that have no resource to the agency of history, only to being historicized in this -cene. Thus to organize a Golden Spike repressing those geologic relations that have carried it socially is to reproduce the ongoing violence of those relations. I want to think about the impaled flesh while maintaining an attention to the refusal to reproduce that racial violence as the only possible position of Blackness thereby producing Blackness and Indigeneity as a negative dialectic to White Geology.

The Golden Spike is not an abstract spike; it is an inhuman instantiation that touches and ablates human and nonhuman flesh, inhuman materials and experiences. It rides through the bodies of a thousand million cells; it bleeds though the open exposure of toxicity, suturing deadening accumulations through many a genealogy and geology. This is the alienation of geology. The fabulation of beginnings in the Anthropocene is tied to the present and its politics, but it also places emphasis on the certain continuities that structure experience from the vantage point of Western colonialism and its ongoing colonial present. Subjects, or rather, modes of subjugation, are also tethered to that event and get erased— modes that continue to reproduce themselves through racialized capitalism in the mines in South Africa and Brazil, right through to the ways in which nuclear fallout is again congressing around the island of Guam, or in the legacies of slavery through incarceration. Because all the proffered Golden Spikes impale flesh, they are sites of violence enacted on the integrity of subjectivity, corporeality, and territoriality. *Origination is displacement.* Each moment of the proposed origin stories of the Anthropocene is as colonial displacement, a migration through events that is disproportionally harbored by people of color and indigenous communities. In the spirit of a speculative geology, which the Anthropocene surely is, given its *geology-in-the-making* and future-oriented explications, considering a fuller social geology would make for a more precise inhuman geology that also addresses the constitutive exclusions of its inhumanity.

Paying attention to the quotidian inhuman social geologies that underpin these geologic acts of spiking would enact a far more revolutionary paradigm shift in the geographies of the Anthropocene. The centrality of race to the production of humanity in the Anthropocene requires a reconfiguration of the subject at the center of white liberal ethical accounts and an acknowledgment of the role of race in the production of the global spaces that constitute the Anthropocene. I want to make several propositions about the inscription of coloniality into the Anthropocene:

1. Anthropocenic discourse enacts a foundational global inscription of race in the conception of humanity that is put forth as an object of concern in the Anthropocene. Moving toward the idea of a billion Black Anthropocenes spotlights that which is already centered in the Anthropocene—race—and would refuse the structural Whiteness of the Anthropocene in its current formation, potentially toward other, more accountable, decolonized, geosocial futures. This is why the formulation is (after Silva) *toward* the idea of a billion Black Anthropocenes and not posed as an alter-cene, in any of its guises as Capitalocene, Chulthocene, Plantationocene, and so on. An idea of a Black Anthropocene poses the question as a redescription of the Anthropocene through the racializing assemblage from which it emerged, rather than claiming a space for Blackness within or outside the Anthropocene (which it is not my place to do precisely because of the colonial histories that have scripted and described the terms of Blackness). This would be to acknowledge how the pursuit of geology made race a technology at its inception. In making the suggestion of an idea of Black Anthropocenes, I am not advocating ontological differentiation as a supplement to Western knowledge practices of modernity to "unsettle" them, or as a corrective lens upon them, to "appropriate non-hegemonic positions for . . . white introspection" (Broeck and Junker 2014, 10). There can be no address of the planetary failures of modernism or its master-subject, Man, without a commitment to overcoming extractive colonialism. Attending to the *economy of flesh* that underpins geologic practices is to attend

to an ongoing moment of origination and natal alienation, a geo-physics of flesh that is Black and Brown.

2. A material and temporal *solidarity* exists between the inscriptions of race in the Anthropocene and the current descriptions of subjects that are caught between the hardening of geopolitical borders and the material destratification of territory. McKittrick argues that "we might re-imagine geographies of dispossession and racial violence not through the comfortable lenses of insides/outsides or us/them, which repeat what Gilmore (2007, 241) calls 'doomed methods of analysis and action,' but as sites through which 'co-operative human efforts' can take place and have a place" (McKittrick 2011, 960). These Anthropocene sites in which various forms of fossilization are being enacted—mining, extraction, waste, extinction—are all geosocial sites of coproduction in which shared histories unfold within deeply unequal power relations. Within this context, the practices that constitute the contemporary Anthropocene-in-the-making and *its* stratifications are a product of, and reinforce, colonial divisions of power, territory, and life. Decolonization matters precisely at this moment because there is a parallel deterritorialization of material environments because of Anthropocenic processes that are compounding the (ongoing) displacement of indigenous peoples (such as in the Arctic, the Pacific, and the Marshall Islands).

3. Judith Butler (2015, 12) describes ethics as a relational description: "The ethical does not primarily describe conduct or disposition, but characterizes a way of understanding the relational framework within which sense, action, and speech become possible [a space of discourse]. The ethical describes a structure of address in which we are called upon to act or to respond in a specific way." The ethical structure of address enacted in Anthropocene discourse should not be about a morality tale of a good or bad Anthropocene (such as that put forward by ecomodernists) but about the relational redescription of the racial mattering and spatial practices within and through geologic relations (i.e., geology and geologic force need to be posed in all their territorial implications and subjective modes). The consecration of the "event" of geology needs to be placed in its proper historic material and symbolic relation to permanently destabilize the geologic monuments of the Anthropocene and their version of historicizing

planetary relations. In a broader geontological frame, this would elucidate the fantasy of origins and the sedimentation of those stories as a structural axis of territorial belonging and subjective power. If, according to Hartman (2003, 185), "the slave occupies the position of the unthought," then the slave also represents geology's afterthought, insomuch as the thirst for geologic materials unleashed certain notions of what and who could be a subject (and in parallel, what and who could be inhuman as both property and possessing valuable properties to be extracted). From the position of the unthought, Hartman asks, "What does it mean to try to bring that position into view without making it a locus of positive value, or without trying to fill the void" (185), without trying to integrate the position into a project founded on anti-Blackness and "investment in certain notions of the subject and subjection" (185)? The Anthropocene is a project initiated and executed through anti-Blackness and inhuman subjective modes, from 1492 to the present, and it cannot have any resolution through individuated liberal modes of subjectivity and subjugation. In short, that world must end for another relation to the earth to begin.

In the skin of a differently narrated geology, we get a broken event, subjects that have emerged through and in that break (to paraphrase Fred Moten) and survived despite the genocidal rage directed at them (which goes way beyond the harnessing of surplus value). Then, we have a billion Black Anthropocenes, an "Undercommons" in Moten's and Harney's words, that already has its own Poethical tradition (in Silva's words, that has a different matter relation). It is a different origin story that has never had the luxury of origins, a "nonoriginal origin" in Sexton's (2010, 41) words. This absent present in the narrative arc of the story of the "Geology of Mankind" is fractured all the way down its fault lines, through the rocks and the earth. Rifted, it has borne the mobilization and militarization of the strata and has lived the Anthropocene as a condition of survival. To quote Moten (2003, 14), "it's the ongoing event of an antiorigin and an anteorigin, replay and reverb of an impossible natal occasion . . . that (dis)establishes genesis." Epochal thinking requires shattering its colonial legacy and the articulation of the fragmentary effects of its ruptures on the "wretched of the earth" (Fanon 1963):

> *My name is Bordeaux and Nates and Liverpool and New York and San*
> *   Francisco*
> *not a corner of this world but carries my thumb-print*
> *and my heel-mark on the backs of skyscrapers and my dirt* (Césaire [1956]
> *   1969, 29–30)*

Césaire continues, naming the geologies of racialized earth, concluding,

> *Red earth, blood earth, blood brother earth (29–30)*

The Inhumanities

To produce Blackness is to produce a social link of subjection
and a body of extraction, that is, a body entirely exposed to the
will of the master, a body from which great effort is made to
extract maximum profit. An exploitable object . . .

—ACHILLE MBEMBE, *A Critique of Black Reason*

If we plumb the depths, then what we will find is fundamentally
black . . . [it is] a process of disalienation. . . . I felt that beneath
the social being would be found a profound being, over whom all
sorts of ancestral layers and alluviums had been deposited.

—AIMÉ CÉSAIRE, *Discourse on Colonialism*

Questions of origin are never too far away from questions of difference and belonging and the various bifurcations of the human
into its subcategories of fully human, subhuman, and inhuman.
Origins also nurture; they grow an armature for narratives; they
root a set of emplacements or belongings into place. Origins are
like the importation of flora and fauna that settlers brought with
them to remake their home. The unsettled had to negotiate origins, too (the voiding of origins that the Middle Passage initiated), making home in no home, taking root, a "replantation"
(Wynter, n.d.) in a slave plot, where growing things is both a narrative and biophysical act. The natal alienation that is established
through the inscription of the inhuman as a subject position within slavery and the dispossession of land that renders the indigenous as subhuman has consequences for how lineage is inscribed

in territory and legitimating rights are established over that territory. The inheritance of ideal subjecthood that is tied to material accumulation vis-à-vis the white patriarchal family continues in the present (Sharpe 2016b). As Hartman (2003) comments, "family values support a eugenics agenda—the reconstitution of the white bourgeois family" (196) where "racial domination and racial abjection are produced across generations" (198). The genealogical arrangements that are used to understand the architecture of Anthropocene origin stories have consequences for the contemporary politics of place. As Brand (2001, 64) argues, "country, nation, these concepts are of course deeply indebted to origins, family, tradition, home. Nation-states are configurations of origins as exclusionary power structures which have legitimacy based solely on conquest and acquisition." The manufacturing of origins is a need and tyranny of the nation, which is predicated on extraction and exploitation. Black and brown death is the precondition of every Anthropocene origin story, and the *grammar* and *graphia* of this geology compose a regime for producing contemporary subjects and subtending settler colonialism. Thus Anthropocene origin stories are broadly concerned not just with geological markers but with a genealogy that inscribes a historicity onto the planet and thereby constitutes the filiation of what and who gets to constitute the historical event.

Origins are not solely about geography. They pertain to the question of how matter is understood and organized, as both extractable resource and energy, mobilized through dehumanizing modes of subjection and conjoining the property and properties of matter in such a way that it collapses the body politic of Blackness into the inhuman—wherein a codification in law and labor becomes an epidemiological signature, as Blackness is marked as property and Whiteness is marked as freedom (political and geographical). This transaction is executed in geologic codes of materiality. As Hartman (1997, 115) argues, "the longstanding and ultimate affiliation of liberty and bondage made it impossible to envision freedom independent of constraint or personhood and autonomy separate from the society of property and proprietorial notions of self." Destabilizing the origin (and originality in general) counters the social reproduction of the relation of race that is established through this geologic ordering of property and proprietorial subjectivity. Slavery provided a "natural" ordering principle in the *technē* of race (Hartman 1997, 121), and Geology's discriminatory classificatory system of property and properties no less participated in the transformation of land relations and extractive economies—a geometry of power that executed dispossession and displacement under the rubric of extraction. The metamorphosis is of geology into slavery or "chattel into man" (Hartman 1997, 111).

While the roles of "natural categories" of race, blood, racial taxonomies of eugenics, and environmental determinism have been critically denaturalized, geology remains stubbornly resilient in maintaining its inhuman categories of metal, gold, mud, slave, earth, Carib. The inscription of geologic principles in the founding narrative of the colonial state, in terms of the colonization of both resources and racialized belonging, encodes the brutal calculative logic of inhuman materiality as a praxis for dispossession that only later acquires its ideological forms, such as "Manifest Destiny." There is a parallel between the languages of the dispossession of subjects and land within the context of the inhuman (and its inhumanities). There was a reliance on both the fixity of geologic description to facilitate exchange (gold, slave, Gold Coast) and its porosity, which enabled a range of different materials to be mobilized within a single system despite differences in sentience, location, and affiliation. In this chapter, I explore the structural antagonisms in the designation of the inhuman in its double sense (as material experience and epistemic "category mistake") and the resistances and refusals in response to this mineralogical intimacy.

Categories of Matter

Geology is a category and praxis of dispossession. It has determined the geographies and genealogies of colonial extraction in a double sense: first, in terms of settler colonialism and the *thirst* for land and minerals, and second, as a category of the inhuman that transformed persons into things. This pincer movement of geology displaces territory as earth and the territory of subjective possession. This is the filiation of "red earth, blood earth, blood brother earth."

Geology as the Space of Transaction

> **Laws of property** a. a thing belonging to someone, things, belonging, goods, chattels. b. an attribute, quality or characteristic of something.

Property Relations

Slave capture and ownership were initially instigated to mine for gold in the New World. Both enslaved, land and ecologies became subject to encoding as inhuman property, as a tactic of empire and European world building. Gold and silver extracted from mines in the Americas flowed to buoy up European markets. The property lines of empire instigated and marked Blackness as both a consequence of labor requirements and a possibility of capital accumulation through geologic extraction. As Wilderson suggests, "one could say that the possibility of becoming property is one of the essential elements that draws the line between blackness and whiteness" (quoted in Hartman 2003, 188). The historic confluence of the science of recognition, identification, and extraction of geologic materials and the establishment of a color line that policed the border in claims to human freedom organized the language of geology beyond the realms of a material science. As Catherine Hall (2014, 28) puts it, "black racial identity marked those who were enslaved. White marked those who were free." Blackness was named as a property of "natal alienation" (which is also genealogical and geographical isolation) and its continuance in social and sexual orders through the enclosure of property relations across all binds of relation. It

> had its counterpoint in the naming of whiteness as a different kind of property—access to public and private privileges, the possibility of controlling critical aspects of one's own life rather than being the object of others' domination. A set of assumptions, privileges and benefits were attached to being white in colonial society that became legitimated, affirmed and protected by law. (28)

Blackness was a legal code and an epidemiological mode of identification that fixed a body politic of Blackness as transportable property to be continuously dis-placed across different geographies and psychic registers across the "door of no return" (Brand 2001; Hartman 2007). Moreover, Whiteness became established as a *right to* geography, to *take* place, to *traverse* the globe and to *extract* from cultural, corporeal, and material registers.

While the accumulation from planter capital was one register of extraction, the accumulation from the violence of *taking place* across multiple registers of belonging was another. The very fungiblity of the commodity allowed Blackness to become mobilized as an ontological possibility within inhuman categories, but conversely, the carceral logic of geologic grammars renders Blackness as flesh, matter, and subject position. The fantasy was to assert commodity value of persons through the rendering of a nonagentic materiality (flesh) to generate surplus value, thereby disfiguring the black subject. Hartman argues that the slave is the essential subject as object, an object to whom anything can be done. The first step in this process of dehumanization is the metamorphosis of human into inhuman thing. The discipline of geology is intrinsic to this structural inscription of subjects into matter-objects or property. Compartmentalization and categorization of matter produce the fungibility of the slave as "thing" and the grammar of "thingification." In a Kentucky slave pen, reconstructed in the National Underground Railroad Freedom Center in Cincinnati, Ohio, an iron ring hangs from the central beam, the one feature in an otherwise empty space. A video playing outside says that the iron ring was "the only human thing in there." The ring formed by a human hand from the inhuman earth, beaten into shape in the forge, maintained in violence by free human hands, hooked so many into inhuman bondage—a bondage that ricochets across the Middle Passage, through so many inhumanities, in infinite arrears. "Here, walls ate skin, footsteps took the mind" (Brand 2001, 224). This fungibility, Hartman argues, is both the breach in natal possibility that leaves subjects unable to access any positionality outside of the codification of Blackness as inhuman property and what organizes the possibility of the interchangeable exchange as a set of properties.

Properties

Both the enslaved and minerals are recognized as possessing certain properties or qualities, namely, energy, reproducibility, and transformation. As Hartman (1997, 26) argues, "the fungibility of the commodity, specifically its abstractness and immateriality, enabled the black body or blackface mask to serve as the vehicle of white self-exploration, renunciation, and enjoyment." The properties of the enslaved "are ontologized as the innate capacities" of the slave property (26). These innate capacities are properties to be worked and channeled, likened to the band of iron that made the ring that held the slaves. These properties for extraction and labor are also tied to the social reproduction of Whiteness; through forced reproduction and rape of the enslaved (or, in Hartman's words, subjection to desire without consent); and in the use of extracted energy for generating the organization of economies of valuation. The instigation of slavery was prompted by a recognition of the so-called properties of African physiology, where indigenous Indians were viewed as not robust enough for mining and plantation work. What is apparent is that the slave and the mineral are recognized in regimes of value, but only so much as they await extraction (where Whiteness is the arbiter and owner of value).

Both these modes of extracting value—as *property* and *properties*—generate surplus. It is the grammar of geology—the inhuman—that establishes the stability of the object of property for extraction. The process of geologic materialization in the making of matter as value is transferred onto subjects and transmutes those subjects through a material and color economy that is organized as ontologically different from the human (who is accorded agency in the pursuits of rights, freedom, and property). The codification of Blackness through the inhuman meant that "there was no relation to blackness outside the terms of this use of, entitlement to, and occupation of the captive body, for even the status of free blacks was shaped and compromised by the existence of slavery" (Hartman 1997, 24). While Hartman argues that property was how the color line was drawn, what is important about her argument is the way in which she demonstrates how the black body becomes a "property of enjoyment" as well as of labor, violence, energy, and so on. The actual body of the slave as an object of identification is always being made to disappear, whether through the optics of pleasure, empathy, or violence, in much the same way as the black or brown body does in the "point and erase" stories of the Anthropocene.

Thus geology was ontologically configured long before the pronouncement of the Anthropocene that designates a "new" geologic identity for humanity. Identification of properties of value and the recognition of property relations to substantiate that theft were the primary drivers of profitability in the colonial context. At the heart of this enterprise was geology as an epistemological discipline and a technology for extraction, settlement, and displacement. The organization of matter and subjects within descriptions that served as a mode of containment produced the very idea of a standing stock of gold, energy, and slaves, organized, as they were, as concomitant categories on a bill of sale. Blackness is rendered as an empty signifier, like gold, silver, and other precious minerals, where the valuation of exchange is established through descriptive markers and subjects are considered as a set of properties (exchange value = type [sex, size, age] + properties [skill, future surplus]). Rights of property are established as a configuration of what is identifiable as value and a mode of possession. As Spillers (2003, 208) argues, "the captive body, then, brings into focus a gathering of social realities as well as a metaphor for value so thoroughly interwoven in their literal and figurative emphases that distinctions between them are virtually useless." Objectification is enacted to deaden subjectivity (and relationality to place). This is how the inhuman as a mode of categorization and a monstrous attitude toward the enslaved contains, regulates, and subjugates bodies. The classification of the inhuman as inert, ahistorical, nonpolitical, inorganic, is both a division of matter that is biopolitical and a regime of ordering matter that separates spheres of politics and agency—or, biopolitics achieved through geologic means.

Who then is objectified by geology's grammar of materiality? Who are its social subjects and kin? What is the ground and relation of these subjects to the earth? Noticing the slide between persons and materials that are consigned to the category of inhuman is not to dispossess further those that have been rendered as inhuman in that configuration; rather, it is to understand the slide between categories and its resistance. Understanding the instability of the category of the inhuman and its stickiness to abject forms of subjecthood opens an examination into how these attachments were facilitated (and continue to be facilitated). Recognizing how the inhuman slips, how the inhuman is made to slide over personhood as a process of making the subjugated (as in the black body rendered as flesh and units of energy), is an unrecognized dynamic of geologic life that rewrites a radically different text for the Anthropocene.

While rewriting the Anthropocene is not of central importance in and of itself (i.e., as an epistemic exercise), the modes of geologic subjectivity that are imagined, and the relation of these ideas of geologic subjectivity to regimes of extraction, are. Understanding how modes of subjectivity are established as categories of extraction is a historic shift in the narrative of world making and a redress of how modes of subjectivity are formed in relation to one another (i.e., the making of chattel as an indifferent category of subject description is tied to the possibility of the possessive liberal individual and white patriarchal family). It is only at the level of the symbolic that the substitutions between Black and Gold can be mobilized as material registers that travel across a monolithic ground. Only through a shift of the axis of sense that allows this transaction (at a material and symbolic level) can a different possibility be enacted to trouble this geophysics predicated on the deformation of brown and black bodies. Looked at through the lens of geology and slavery, the descriptive opacity of the Anthropocene as a reckoning with geologic relations seems disingenuous. For the displacement from land and ecologic relation that form the possibility of place are covered over, and subjective life is tied to the instigation of chattel slavery (which is coded in parallel with material extraction). It is the very codes and grades of inhuman matter as they are generically applied to minerals that become reconstituted in the generic slave codes (of property and properties). While the recognition of material properties of colonized land in terms of extractable properties drives the colonial imperative and its need for slave labor, the slave becomes an effect of that extractive grammar and its embodiment and resistance.

In twining the traffic between the inhuman and inhumane, the presumed neutrality of geology as a mode of description is disrupted. Blackness is displaced and effaced in the pursuit of value for Western colonialism through and as extraction. Geologic principles are used to establish a biocentrism that delineates from the human to subhuman to inhuman, as a property relation and as a mark of agentic properties. It is not that geology is productive of race per se but that empirical processes mesh across geological propositions and propositions of racial identity to produce an equation of inhuman property as racially coded. This dynamic of disinheritance (and white inheritance) is ideologically maintained through the notions of species in geologic time. As Fanon (1963, 39) argued, "this world divided into compartments, this world cut in two is inhabited by two different species. . . . When you examine at close quarters the colonial context, it is evident that what parcels out the world is to begin with the fact of belonging to or not belonging to a given race, a given species." It is equally true that the optics of belonging to a given race is the *technē* of origination that is invented to parcel out the earth.

"The Principles of Geology"

Sir Charles Lyell, president of the Geological Society of London and author of *The Principles of Geology* (a text that directly informed Darwin's ideas of evolution), makes clear the ways in which geology and racial propositions are intertwined in his published accounts of his geologic surveying of North America (Lyell 1845, 1849). Eclectic in a manner that must have been familiar to his audiences, he moves in between "Geology and Cretaceous strata" and "Montgomery. Curfew. Sunday School for Negros" in one chapter (chapter XXII) and "Distinct Table for Coloured and White Passengers" and "Fossil Shells" (Lyell 1849, chapter XXIII) in another. The ledger for chapter IX reads, "Return to Charleston—Fossil Human Skeleton—Species of Shells common to Eocene Strata in America and Europe—Condition of Slave Population—Cheerfulness of the Negroes: their Vanity—State of Animal Existence—Invalidity of marriages—The Coloured Population multiply faster than the Whites—Effects of the interference of Abolitionists." Lyell's speculations on race are firmly underpinned by the language he has forged for geology, as he defines the problems of the races and their respective (as he understands them) positions in relation to time, in much the same way as his descriptions of geology define the stratification of rock formations and species in time. That is, the Negro is understood by Lyell as a different species in time than "the White." Notwithstanding his concerns over the population growth of Negroes and the subsequent effect on the white race, both racially and economically, Lyell (1849, 95) suggests, "I shall cherish the most sanguine hopes

of their future improvement and emancipation, and even their ultimate amalgamation and fusion with the whites, so highly has my
estimate of their moral and intellectual capabilities been raised by
what I have lately seen in Georgia and Alabama." While Lyell's pa-
ternalist opinion seems to have been bolstered by an invigorating
sermon in a Negro church, where he praises the lyricism of the
Negroes and how they have embraced his understanding of moral
progress, his representation of the problem of the race is directly
informed by his account of the principles of geology (and the notion of improvement and gradualism that framed his account of
geologic formations). As the table of contents attests, he sees no
difference in the crossings between social and geologic strata with
regard to the language of property and possibility across fossil objects and Negroes.

On the question of emancipation, Lyell quotes an advocate from
the North, reasoning that if emancipation were not granted, then
the Negro population would grow to outnumber the White population. He says, "But would not the progress of the whites be re-
tarded, and our race deteriorated, nearly in the same proportion
as the negroes would gain? Why not consider the interests of the
white race by hastening the abolition of slavery. The whites constitute nearly six-sevenths of our whole population. As a philan-
thropist, you are bound to look at the greatest good of the two races collectively" (Lyell 1849, 101). More than a hundred years later,
James Baldwin debates at Cambridge University Union with the
conservative right-wing author William F. Buckley on a motion
that is both the child of this question of the progress of Whites
and its inversion: "Has the American Dream been achieved at the
expense of the American Negro?" In his statement, Baldwin exposes the hypocrisies of liberalism and tears apart the notion of
progress when one-ninth of the population is excluded. Toward
the end of his speech, Baldwin declared that until it was accepted
that "I am not a ward of America," a subject of pity and charity, but
instead that "I am one of the people who built the country—until
this moment comes there is scarcely any hope for the American

dream."[1] What Lyell addresses as the issue of progress, as a system of reality that is produced through a temporal geologic formulation, Baldwin is still challenging a century later.

Lyell (1845) states the social work of temporal formations explicitly when he says, "To inspire them with an aptitude for rapid advancement must be the work of time—the result of improvement carried on through several successive generations. *Time is precisely the condition* for which the advocates of the immediate liberation of the blacks would never sufficiently allow" (191–92, emphasis added). Employing the notion of "Times Arrow" (later made famous by another geologist, Stephen Jay Gould), Lyell makes the symbolic offering of time and its possibilities for freedom and then represses that possibility through a generational requirement, so that Blackness is always belated in time and therefore never fully now and human. Wright suggests that "the tendency to misread this Blackness as a 'what' imposes even more the fixity so that Blackness, as a vaguely biological 'what' takes on an eerie resemblance to those anti-Black discourses that first claimed Blacks were indeed a 'what'—a distinct subspecies 'marked by nature,' as Jefferson opined" (Wright 2015, 25). The "what" of Blackness was rendered through the lexicon of the inhuman. Only geologic time, according to Lyell, would allow for the transformation of what into who.

As in answer to the legacy of Lyell's thinking and its multiple manifestations through the generations of the Jim Crow era,

---

1. The black feminist Audre Lorde (1984) challenges Baldwin's attachment to the American dream as a patriarchal instantiation: "Deep, deep, deep down I know that dream was—never mine. . . . Nobody was studying me except as something to wipe out. . . . Even worse than the nightmare is the Blank. And Black women are the blank. . . . We have to admit and deal with difference. . . . If we can put people on the moon and we can blow this whole planet up, if we can consider digging 18 inches of radioactive dirt off the Bikini atolls and somehow finding something to do with it—if we can do that, we as Black cultural workers can somehow begin to turn that stuff around."

Baldwin, in the 1989 documentary *The Price of a Ticket,* challenges
the idea that racial progress needs to "take time." He says, "What is
it you want me to reconcile myself to? I was born here nearly sixty
years ago, I'm not going to live another sixty years, you always tell
me it takes time. It's taken my father's time, my mother's time, my
uncle's, my brother's and my sister's time, my niece's and my neph-
ew's time, how much time do you want for your progress? The cut
with which Baldwin spits out the word progress is clean to the
bone. Nina Simone sings it in 'Mississippi Goddam' (1964), in response to the murder of Medgar Evans and the 16th Street Baptist
Church bombing in Birmingham, Alabama that killed four black
children, 'Too slow'; 'Keep on sayin' 'go slow.' . . . to do things grad-
ually would bring more tragedy. Why don't you see it? Why don't
you feel it? I don't know, I don't know. You don't have to live next
to me, just give me my equality!" As Mbembe (2017, 17) argues,
"the notion of race made it possible to represent non-European
human groups as trapped in a lesser form of being. They were the
impoverished reflection of the ideal man, separated from him by
an insurmountable temporal divide, a difference nearly impossible to overcome." Locked into a belatedness in becoming human
enough in relation to the ideal (white) humanist subject, the spati-
alizing of time along a vertical line is used as a mechanism to deny
juridical rights, wherein Whiteness becomes the achievement of
one's temporal identity in geologic time.

In the presumption of what needs to be explained about slavery,
a geohistorical horizon is established into which questions of race
and possibility are staged as self-evidently differentiated in time,
to justify subjection and material dispossession (from intimate
kin and sexual relations to the ownership of land). Lyell's whim-
sical speculations point to how these geological underpinnings of
the rubric of property, paternalism, and moral economy establish
modes of subjectification as thoroughly sedimented in the bedrock
of geology and its categorizing of fossil objects in time. The figure
of the Negro is the substantive subject of this historicization that
figures the question of race within and through geological classi-

fications and its descriptive modes of extractive *pre*configuration. The construction of the human as such, as it pertains to origins, is divided along with geologic strata into White and Negro as part of the differentiating discourse of race and time, in which Whiteness signals arrival and Blackness belatedness. Lyell (1845, 191) says,

> I am by no means disposed to assume that the natural capacities of the negroes, who always appeared to me to be an amiable, gentle, and inoffensive race, may not be equal in a moral and intellectual point of view to those of the Europeans, provided the coloured population were placed in circumstances equally favourable for their development. But it would be visionary to expect that, under any imaginable system, this race could at once acquire as much energy, and become as rapidly progressive, as the Anglo-Saxons.

When Lyell tries to justify this carceral lacuna in time, he comes up with a transcendental categorical distinction across generations, where the teleological principles of thought take a presumption of the "unimaginable" as a principle. Yet, there is a slippage in this description of the unimaginable acquisition of "as much energy" which allows progression, in that it names the theft of energy that is slavery as the propulsion of white evolutionary achievement. As a slow converter to the idea of the transmutation of the species through Darwin's concept of natural selection, Lyell was suspicious of the possibility for change, preferring to see the relations between races (as with geology) as defined by gradual transformation and the impact of favorable conditions (understood by him as both social and climatic). Geology becomes a way to frame the unfolding progression of liberal teleology. He says,

> They cannot be fused at once into the general mass, and become amalgamated with the whites, for their colour still remains as the badge of their former bondage, so that they continue, after their fetters are removed, to form a separate and inferior caste. How long this state of things would last must depend on their natural capabilities, moral, intellectual, and physical; but if in these they be equal to whites, they would eventually become the dominant race, since the climate of the south, more congenial to their constitutions, would give them decided advantage. (193)

In Lyell's reasoning, Blackness was a monolith that was separated from Whiteness through metaphors of value that are complicated by understandings of the biologic determinism through climate (as a racialized construction). Again, there is the slippage between the categorization of property and its effects and the role of "natural" properties that determine (in Lyell's mind) the environmental possibilities of evolution, and thus a risk to white society. The epistemic violence is doubly enacted: "it touches generations of social formations both over time (transhistorical and memorial) and in time (historical and material)" (Spillers 2003, xiii). Lyell's comments reveal the affective infrastructures that travel under scientific reason that privileges white comfort ("anxiety") over black pain:

> Had the white man never interposed to transplant the negro into the New World, the most generous asserters of the liberties of the coloured race would have conceded that Africa afforded space enough for their development. Neither in their new country, nor in that of their origin, whether in a condition of slavery or freedom, have they as yet exhibited such superior qualities and virtues as to make us *anxious*. (Lyell 1845, 195, emphasis added)

While Lyell's views replicate rather than elucidate any departure from norms in the discussion of slavery, what is important to note is how his argumentation draws on a linear notion of time (see Wright 2015, 37) that is embedded in a biopolitical tale of applying stratigraphic thinking to ideas of cultural and biological progression. This notion of progression is used inversely to excuse and diminish the effect of the forced migration and enslavements of Africans to the Americas. Lyell makes explicit in his discussion on slavery and the interspersion of these discussions through his notes on rocks and mineral resources *how* geology functions as the racial supplement to the progress narrative. This racial supplementarity of geology is not just a material placement in the order of things, but it does psychic work in assuring white anxiety so that recognition of being fully human is forestalled (and thus remains fully exploitable). Lyell's anxiety read in reverse shows that what allows white self-actualization (or comfort) is slavery.

Spillers (2003, xiii) writes that "material values engender symbolic and discursive ones (vice-versa) in perfect synecdochic harmony." This emplacement of the slave within geologic orders demonstrates the racial encoding of political life (*bios*) in slavery through the categories of matter and its properties before it becomes ideologically sedimented in a discourse of racialized biology. Yet, there is a biopolitical disjuncture between the description of geology and its corporeal affects that produces a monstrous impolitic materiality. Rather, geologic time provides the context for the formation of the privileged biocentric subject. The organization and categorization of materiality enact a praxis of colonialism or a taxonomy of race that is productive of racial logics that extend through and beyond mineralogy and its extractions. The ancestry of human beings is not to be always and entirely conflated with work on the development of species but origins of human–animal filiation are part of the story that frames the development of both the geologic and biological sciences. The context of slavery and the practices of geology as an extractive science provide a co-constituting fabric to colonial enterprise and the projects of description of both the earth and the "place" of different humans within it. That is, perceptions of social formations and geologic organizations are linked through both practices and sets of ideas/ideals. In the context of the propulsion of species narrative as the survival of all in the Anthropocene, this cozy, "innocent" universal of geologic realism reinforces the idea of matter as independent of its languages of description rather than as a structuring device of property and properties. Thus it replicates the political and racial divisions of matter even as it obscures them. Geology as colonial mode of classification underwrites the Anthropocene regardless of which settler origin story of the Anthropocene is taken as the moment of origination. If we see the Anthropocene turn to the species thinking as a way to try to save it—in a recuperative mode—this literally requires a writing of the rock (i.e., via a geologically established mode of subjectivity) to achieve the overhaul of human to species via geological epoch. To achieve this ideal of the *Anthropos* as universal subject, the human needs to become both abstracted (from its previous forms of exclusionary humanism) and already populated in the form of the White Western master-subject whom Sylvia Wynter calls "Over Represented Man."

Geology is a mechanism of power and statecraft that has a lower resolution or a more subterranean subjective operation than more performative biopolitics, but it nonetheless continues to be repressive in its extraction qualities and sediments the settler-colonial state. This extractive praxis sets up an instrumental relation to land, ecology, and people. If the geosocial relations of Old and New Worlds are put in conversation with their racial formations, the racial nomos of white settler colonialism can be seen to be established through the infrapolitics of geologic relations. Race and its marking through the geologic term of the inhuman upsets the supposed "natural" boundaries of matter in the classification of human/inhuman, estranging both these terms. Whereas we recognize geologic material practices (oil and mineral extraction) as explicitly tied up in the realm of the political, the declared innocence of acts of description and their historical inscriptions on bodies and geographies are left unexamined. Blackness opens up this "scene of subjection" (Hartman 1997) to its historical fault lines, but it also bears on those geoforces in the present, on the "now" of Blackness, and how Blackness is cast in the storms of environmental change. Corporeality is always established in the zone of territoriality as a form of territoriality over and through black subjects, from chattel slavery through ongoing environmental racism, wherein Blackness becomes what could be termed an *ontology without territory.*

The purchase and extension of the territorial *impulse* (to conquer lands for resource extraction and to organize labor forms to mobilize that extraction, while simultaneously severing the bonds of attachment and territory of enslaved peoples) to subjects organize the dual excess of colonialism. Corporeality for black subjects was not established in the zone of ontology but foreshadowed in the zone of territory and its grammars of extraction. Intervening at the level of narrative is not just a redirection of sense and politics—political aesthetics—but a recognition of how those narrative forces shape the possibilities for praxis in contemporary extraction. It is a tactic to secure a territory in the present against the redress of this historic possession and the ways in which properties are cast and traded as fungible in processes of valuation that make them exchangeable. Therefore any attempt at an Anthropocenic universality is not a question of reorganization at the level of ontology, or what could be called the desire for *ontodeliverance,* that is, the idea that a new ontological formation that includes differently situated subjects will change the terms of engagement. The very "matter" of territorial impulse that materially comprised the Anthropocene is anti-Blackness; it is racialized matter that delivers the Anthropocene as a geologic event into the world, through mining, plantations, railroads, labor, and energy. While Blackness is the energy and flesh of the Anthropocene, it is excluded from the wealth of its accumulation. Rather, Blackness must absorb the excess of that surplus as toxicity, pollution, and intensification of storms. Again, and again.

The Division of Matter and Geologic Life

Crisscrossing this caesura between the inhuman and inhuman(e) is a way to talk about the historical forms and contexts of the racialization of matter. The organization and categorization of matter enact racialization. This enactment is productive of racial logics that extend through and beyond mineralogy and the deterritorialization that accompanies extraction. Geology provides the logics to elide those attachments to geography through its classification system of value and resource. While the search for geologic resources instigated the imperative to enslave, geology quickly established itself as an imperial science that both organized the extraction of the Americas and, in the continued context of Victorian colonialism, became a structuring priority in the colonial complex, especially in India, Canada, and Australia. These territories became organized *as* material resources and markets for Empire, and the geologic practices established in these colonies continued to underwrite current neocolonial extraction processes by Canada and Australia throughout the world (Canada, for example, is the largest national global mining corporation). The ownership of strata and the surface–subsurface bifurcation in Australia and Canada by the Crown continue to unsettle native title and reservation lands. Thus the classificatory logics of geology have implications for ongoing colonialism.

Geologic classification enabled the transformation of territory into a readable map of resources and organized the apprehension of extraction and the designation of extractable territories. Geology was the science of material dispossession but also a social technology of naturalization. The motivation of colonialism was as an extraction project. The consequence of this formation of inhuman materialism was the organization of racializing logics that maps onto and locks into the formation of extractable territories and subjects. While the critiqued notion of environmental determinism of the continents provided the basis for accounts of the classification of the races and sedimented race into climatology, the rocks escaped being understood as part of the determination of races. There was a material division made between climate and earth through a property relation. The ideological notion of environmental determinism is historically concurrent with the classification of rocks, but rather than cement the relation between nature and race, geology is used to separate one race (Blackness) from the mineralogical ground while enriching another (Whiteness) through the description and division of matter into a sign and system of containment. Bodies become gold, emptied of the sign of the human, reinvested with the signification of units of energy and properties of extraction. Black is made as will-less matter, a commodity object of labor. This is what Hartman calls the "double bind of agency," where acceptance into the genre of the human is only offered as a further inscription in the terms of labor and its modes of subjectivity. Geology then becomes a spacing in the imagination that is used to separate forms of the human into permissible modes of exchange and circulation. This is the geotrauma of a billion Black Anthropocenes. If geologic relations are to be examined, a radical interrogation must remain as traumatic as its passage.

This chapter has paid attention to the transactions between geology and slavery as a traffic in modes of production and subjection, organized around the grammar of the inhuman. Rather than turning away from this geologic code, Black Poethics (to use Silva's term) has intensified this bond as a release from its bondage to redefine both black subjectivity and "inert" materiality. In her poem *Coal,* Audre Lorde (1996, 6) revisits the essentializing biology of matter in the context of language as a structuring matter-economy, engaging the blackness of coal and its idealized form (diamonds) as an oppositional transmutation (see also Dhairyam 2017; Gumbs 2017):

> *I*
> *Is the total black, being spoken*
> *From the earth's inside.*
> *There are many kinds of open.*
> *How a diamond comes into a knot of flame*
> *How a sound comes into a word, coloured*
> *By who pays what for speaking.*

Turning away from the privileged white subject of biopolitical life, the "I" that Lorde throws her intimacy in with is allied to the inhuman earth. "I/Is the total black" resists the autonomous and individualized subjectification of Whiteness and refuses the inhuman codified as property to embrace the collective subject of Blackness that has been gathered into categories of earth. As Glissant (1997, 9) confirms, "we know ourselves as part and as crowd, in an unknown that does not terrify. We cry our cry of poetry. Our boats are open, and we sail them for everyone." Shifting the terms of participation in humanist models that were born in a scene of anti-Blackness, Lorde offers another "open" that makes a commonality of the filiation of Blackness with the earth. Repowering this inhuman designation through the rocks, spoken from the earth's insides, in the context of their extraction, she asks the crucial question in the generation of value from black bodies and black rocks: *who pays what for the speaking*? In the bold resistance of a given inhuman life, poetry and spatial practices "replant" (in Wynter's words) place, mark another possible inhuman relation that does not replicate the confinements of colonial grammar. Transmutation, metamorphoses, and ideals haunt the graphia and geologies of the black radical tradition. In the next chapter, I turn to this intimacy with the inhuman as an alliance with freedom in the matter and maroonage of imposed lands, to think freedom in the earth, outside and against the world of the "given" humanist subject (and their space-time).

Insurgent Geology: A Billion Black Anthropocenes Now

If, thus, we allow that an aesthetics is an art of conceiving, imagining, acting, the other of thought is the aesthetics implemented by me and by you to join the dynamics to which we are to contribute. This is the part fallen to me in an aesthetics of chaos.

—ÉDOUARD GLISSANT, *Poetics of Relation*

Counting her own theory, the theory of nothing, she had opened up the world. In every city in the Old World are Marie Ursule's New World wanderers real and chimeric. . . . They wander as if they have no century, as if they can bound time . . . compasses whose directions tilt, skid off known maps. . . . They are bony with hope, muscular with grief possession.

—DIONNE BRAND, *A Map to the Door of No Return: Notes to Belonging*

Black Geophysics and the "Unthought" Geoaesthetics of the Earth

Inspired by the work of black feminist scholars—Dionne Brand's poetry about "coming out a woman crushing stones," Sylvia Wynter's ideas from "Black Metamorphosis" on the "senses as theoreticians," and Tina Campt's "quiet aesthetics"—this chapter plots the course of a black geophysics crafted in the indices of fungibility and fugitivity, an aesthetics made in the provisional ground of slavery and its continuing afterlives (Hartman 1997).

Focusing on three fugitive scenes—Steve McQueen's paired films *Carib's Leap/Western Deep* (2002), a print of a slave woman jumping from a window but suspended in a different gravitational field on display at the NMAAHC, and Brand's character Marie Ursule in *At the Full and Change of the Moon* (1999)—I speak to the traffic between the categories of the inhuman in the White Geology of transatlantic slavery and in its Anthropocenic present. These images and Brand's poetry of rocks insist upon what Campt calls futurity through the notion of "tense," to offer an anterior possibility that cuts through coloniality as a counteraesthetic that refuses the inhuman in its codified state as property. Rather, the intimacies with the inhuman forged through "an aesthetics of chaos" are reworked in new poetic grammars to create an insurgent geology of belonging, one that refuses capture by geologic forces and redirects their nonstratified forces as a sense of possibility. These, what Campt calls "quiet acts," might be thought as an "unthought" geophysics of White Geology, which gives another tense to the property and properties relation that emerged through the black hole of slavery, what might be called the black geophysics of "*trans*plantation" (Wynter, n.d.) to a New World.

Wynter uses the term *trans*plantation to reconceptualize how black bodies reclaimed a right to geography within the carceral confines of the plantation and their relocation across the Atlantic. She argues that black culture represented "an alternate way of thought, one in which the mind and the senses coexist, where the mind 'feels' and the senses become theoreticians. And black culture then and now remains the neo-popular, neo-native culture of the disrupted. It coexisted, and coexists, with the 'rational' plantation system, is in constant danger of destruction" (Wynter, n.d., 109). The idea of "senses as theoreticians" establishes how modes of experience are established in sense as a theoretical formulation of subjectivity made in the context of the denial of that subjectivity. This aesthetics or (political affect) is deeply political precisely because it relates to the possibility of life and its survival under conditions of violence. Citing how blues, and its unending part, without climax or end, established time outside of European sense of time and factory time, blues time is taken as space and a subversive territory of place; making of time into space creates territory free from enslaved labor, a counterpoetics, "subterraneanly subversive of its surface reality" (Wynter, n.d., 218). That is, "black oral culture of the New World constituted a counteraesthetic which was at the same time a counter-ethic" (Wynter, n.d., 141). This thinking through sense achieved "the most difficult of all revolutions—*the transformation of psychic state of feeling*" (Wynter, n.d., 245, emphasis original).

Black Aesthetics at the End of the World

In Steve McQueen's film *Caribs' Leap/Western Deep* (2002),[1] two films are paired that tell the story of an act of suicidal escape and collective resistance in Grenada and contemporary gold mining in South Africa. It is a twined story of fugitivity and fungibility, of indigenous genocide and black bodies defined through the property of labor. *Caribs' Leap*'s scene is 1651 Grenada, where the last Indian Caribs chose to jump to their deaths rather than submit to the invading French. It is an event that is said to have occurred at a cliff in the town of Sauteurs, now known as Caribs' Leap. We see the figures always in mid-flight, never jumping or landing but suspended in an endless, ever falling body, gently held by the atmosphere. These figures defy gravity, seemingly floating indefinitely in the sky, never surrendered to the ground, cut alongside an image of a bobbing boat called *Caliban* and the shifting sands on a beach. *Western Deep* was filmed in the TauTona Mine (or Western Deep No. 3 Shaft) in the gold fields of the Witwatersrand Basin near Johannesburg in South Africa. The Western Deep mines are owned by AngloGold Ashanti, part of the international mining con-

1. McQueen's film was screened in the abandoned, subterranean Lumiere cinema in St. Martin's Lane, London, in November 2002.

glomerate Anglo American, and the basin held about 50 percent of all the gold ever mined on earth. The mines in the Witwatersrand Basin are the deepest mines in the world at nearly 3.9 kilometers underground and represent the furthest human bodies go into the earth's depths. The mine employs nearly fifty-six hundred miners, who travel for an hour down the shaft to the rock face, where temperatures can reach up to 140 degrees Fahrenheit. In the deepest parts of the mines, the pressure above the miners is ninety-five hundred tons per meter squared, or approximately 920 times normal atmospheric pressure. The conditions can have serious, life-threatening consequences for the miners.

McQueen's camera follows the shaft down, down into the earth, through dust, in the confined space of the cage, in the sheer near-darkness with a sound that reverberates in the concrete shell of the empty cinema through the tissue to bone. It is the black void of dark out of which nothing seems to emerge; then there is punctuation by an intermittent flicking light that allows a momentary sighting on location in the abyss, only to take us back down into it again. A terrible incessant industrial noise wails, visceral to nerve of teeth, exacting its excruciating assault on the body. After the shaft comes to the surface, the miners, dressed in their blue shorts, perform exercises, exhaustedly stepping up and down on a bench as red buzzers blare above their heads. The heaviness of their bodies on the edge of collapse, unfocused eyes from the dark void, all communicate the living death of their labor and the gravity of two miles of rock on flesh. Structured around the themes of descent, over- and underground, the films speak to a geophysics of anti-Blackness: self-destruction as quotidian subjection and fugitive collective escape. Cutting together gold and Blackness, past and future, McQueen tethers the dual corporeal effects of geology as territorial and psychic dispossession, a process of anti-Blackness that spans the two historical moments from 1651 to 2002. McQueen's figures of ascent and descent draw on his own bibliographical connections to the island and the flying African folklore that drew figures escaping the terror of slavery through a shift of geophysics. Steve McQueen's films together give us the *surrogates of geology*; slavery exposes the subterranean space-time of geology as a psychic and physical space. Sensibility here is not just thinking about exemplars of freedom and slavery but a practice of theorizing of how certain conditions pull and ground subjective possibilities within those twin natalities, possibilities that are infused with the individuation of liberal subjectivity and the collective refusal of that offering in what Glissant calls the "consent not to be a single being."

Refusing the path of self-destruction, either through persistence in the violent property relation or through suicide, "flying Africans" (Synder 2015) was a genre that presented a possibility of "Making a Way Out of No Way" (NMAAHC), an alternative fungibility to the absolute fungibility of black bodies as extraction frontier. This "other gravity" might be thought in Tiffany King's (2016, 1023) analysis of black fungibility as a spatial analytic, where "Black fungibility also functions as a mode of critique and an alternative reading practice that reroutes lines of inquiry around humanist assumptions and aspirations that pull critique toward incorporation into categories like labor(er)." King counters the absolute claim of fungiblity on the black body and its properties, tilting the axis of engagement. She argues that by "theorizing Black bodies as forms of flux or space in process rather than as human producers, stewards and occupiers of space enables at least a momentary reflection upon other kinds of (often forgotten) relationships that Black bodies have to plants, objects, and non-human life forms" (1023). Opening the state of possibility to the transformative intrarelations with other forms of life and nonlife unsettles and redirects the confinements of humanist prescriptions of what and how life is constituted. As King suggests, "black fungibility can also operate as a site of deferral or escape from the current entrapments of the human" (1024). Reclaiming fungibility from the bounded inscriptions of black social death opens and realigns the property–properties relation to speak to time-space coordinates that are not already occupied by the authorizing center, Colonial Man.

In another scene of refusal, Brand's character Marie Ursule, a slave on the island of Trinidad in 1824 in *At the Full and Change of the Moon* (1999), plots a mass suicide as a quiet and defiant act of revolt (based on an actual mass slave suicide in 1802). Marie Ursule gathers the poisons, the potent vines, learned from forging connections to this new earth and its ecologies, from listening to the few Caribs "left alive on the island after their own great and long devastation by the Europeans" (Brand 1999, 2). Faithful to its plants, "she ground the roots to their arresting sweetness, scraped the bark for its abrupt knowledge" (Brand 1999, 2). Marie Ursule alone remains after the mass suicide, awaiting her death by the master, in order to witness his witnessing of this brazen act of wreckage on the plantation economy. Not taking the poison she has prepared, so that she can show them how she had devastated them, she says to the planters, "This is but a drink of water to what I have already suffered" (Brand 1999, 24) as she is beaten, broken, hanged, and burned. After two years with her one foot ringed with ten pounds of iron and the loss of an ear for an earlier attempt at escape, the queen of rebels turns her terror back to its point of origination: the master. After the mass poisoning of the Regiment of San Peur (without fear) society, the end of one world begets another: that of the descendants of Marie Ursule, queen of the San Peur. The morning of the suicide, Marie Ursule sends away her child Bola, and the novel follows her Caribbean diaspora across the geographies of the diaspora itself, from plantation to maroonage, through the centuries to the streets of Toronto and Amsterdam. When the proclamation comes by Sir George Fitzgerald Hill, lieutenant-governor in 1833, to end slavery, Brand displaces this "grudgeful news" that has come too late and admits too much, suggesting that "its authority is surpassed by the authority of Marie Ursule's act ten years ago when she woke up to the end of the world" (51).

Marie Ursule's New World and its genealogy of fragmentation, its wandering and desire, are told through the children of Bola, whose lives in the great fluidity of diaspora parallel the fluidity of the air and matter and rocks. Marie Ursule is remembered in the gathered impulses left in bones, in lives that spill over in the new world coming, "gestures muscular with dispossession" (Brand 1999, 20). Whereas slavery enacted terror, in Hartman's (2007, 40) terms, "terror was 'captivity without the possibility of flight,' inescapable violence, precarious life. There was no going back to a time or place before slavery, and going beyond it no doubt would entail nothing less momentous that yet another revolution." Such a revolution is exacted in the refusal of Marie Ursule through her quotidian relations with plant and geologic life that form an otherwise, which refutes the inhuman constitution of the fungible relation through the fugitivity of dispossession. The impossible becomes possible through a shift in the exchanges of inhuman fungibility. Overwriting the capacity for nonbeing in the diaspora, Brand's materiality of language establishes the presentness of Blackness and makes that presentness an obligation with which to counter its erasure. Her poetry speaks the fungibility of the black body as flooded with the world. The earth, the weather, the ocean, and the tides and its materiality have a life in the work and world. It is a materiality that cuts through coloniality as a counteraesthetic, a poetry of rocks that tells a different story of rocks.

Brand's writing finds, haunts, and nudges against another image of a woman leaping, sleep walking, escaping, held in the suspension between fungibility and fugitivity. A woman is suspended out the window in an 1817 print at the NMAAHC. The text reads that she jumped out of the window after the sale of her husband and that she survived the fall. The wind catches and balloons her dress, but she is not falling. She has a different field of gravity that is held by a barely perceptible planetary shift in the allegiances of matter: "The problem was gravity and the answer was gravity" (Brand 2014, 157). She both escaped out the window and is not yet returned to the exposure of her captivity through the forces that would return her to the earth. The image possesses something of what Campt (2017, 5) calls the quiet amplification of "rupture and refusal." In the geophysics of this image of the suspended woman,

Courtesy of the American Antiquarian Society.

gravity is both the problem and the solution, rendering her invulnerable, held in the possible, awaiting a different tense of being. A different future. In another era, in the 1983 American invasion of Grenada, another woman is forced into conflict with the weight of this historical gravity of colonialism:

> She jump. Leap from me. Then I decide to count the endless names of stones. Rock leap, wall heart, rip eye, cease breadth, marl cut, blood leap, clay deep, coal dead, coal deep, never rot, never cease, sand high, bone dirt, dust hard, mud bird, mud fish, mud word, rock flower, coral water, coral heart, coral breath. . . .
>
> She's flying out to sea and in the emerald she sees the sea, its eyes translucent, its back solid going to some place so old there's no memory of it. She's leaping. She's tasting her own tears and she is weightless and deadly. She feels nothing except the bubble of a laugh each time she breathes. Her body is cool, cool in the air. Her body has fallen away, it just a line, an electric current, the sign of lightning left after lightening, a faultless arc to the deep turquoise deep. She doesn't need air. She's in some other place already, less tortuous, less fleshy. (Brand 1996, 241–42, 246–47)

In these images of another gravity, the printmaker and poet have, in Campt's (2017, 17) words, strived "for the tense of possibility that grammarians refer to as the future real conditional or *that which will have had to happen*." A woman is waiting, suspended above the earth in a different gravity. In the grammar of black feminist futurity, it is

> a performance of a future that hasn't yet happened but must. It is an attachment to a belief in what should be true, which impels us to realize that aspiration. It is power to imagine beyond current fact and to envision that which is not, but must be. It's a politics of prefiguration that involves living the future *now*—as imperative rather than subjunctive—as a striving for the future you want to see, right now, in the present. (Campt 2017, 17)

If the woman who is fleeing out of the window is given an escape route that matches her own claim to possession of her body by the printmaker, her survival is doubly given in a disruptive grammar of geology; she has unbound herself in the very same language of matter that would make a person into a thing, defying the weight of her flesh arranged in the matter of anti-Blackness.

Hartman urges an attentiveness to how Blackness is made captive. Any recourse to the release of that captivity in descriptive moments of transgression that are held up as agency should be treated with caution in the "tragic continuities between slavery and freedom." Imagining and representing scenes of "freedom" within slavery, a kind of hopeful overcoming, negates the way in which freedom and its conceptual apparatus were built on that subjection, with slavery very much in mind. That is, humanity was never for the whole of humanity, and freedom was only for some and a systemic regulation (and literal reproduction) of slavery for others. There is no recuperation of the captive or the captured in terms of agency within these positions and their legacy in the afterlife of slavery, because there is never the possibility of consent Hartman argues. The Black Anthropocenes or None is thus already a priori null and void. Drawing attention to a billion Black Anthropocenes is not a vehicle of visibility to see the dark underbelly of modernity with greater clarity, because it is already erased and caught in the process of erasure. So "Blackness" and "Slave" could be added to the ledger of Lewis and Maslin's diagram of New World exchange as the *sub-* or *sur*text of racial difference and extraction, but that would do nothing to ameliorate that this was not an exchange by any conception of the imagination, only an "X" that marks the absence of that possibility. Slavery and genocide are the *ur*text to discussions of species and geology, their empirical bedrock and epistemic anchor. Another way to say this is that escape from captivity is only possible within the indices of that grammar of captivity and its interstitial moments, never as idealized outside of it. The deformation of inhuman subjectivity is made from within that matter, and so is its refusal and aesthetics of resistance. That is, to paraphrase Campt (2017, 59), to reread refusal not necessarily as "an inextricable expression of agential intention" but as a muscular refashioning, "bony with hope." The destabilization of the inhuman as a category of chattel into an atmospheric, environmental sense and geophysical "tense" (Campt 2017) repositions the "event" in a different idea of time, space, and matter, an affective environment made through altered categories of description or aesthetics of the inhuman.

The colonial inscription that overwrites the inhuman as property and properties and its parallel geologies of displacement are aptly articulated by Brand (1997) in *Land,* written in the rifts of this geologic reason. She says, "Written as wilderness, wood, nickel, water, coal, rock, prairie, erased as Athabasca, Algonquin, Salish, Inuit . . . hooded in Buxton fugitive, Preston Black Loyalist, railroaded to gold mountain, swimming to *Komagata Maru.* . . . Are we still moving? Each body submerged in its awful history. When will we arrive?" (77). The places of Athabasca, Algonquin, Salish, Inuit, become "wilderness," nickel, coal, prairie, commodities to be extracted. The Buxton community of black Canadians in Ontario, descendants of freed and fugitive slaves who escaped via the Underground Railroad; the "gold mountain" on the continental divide of British Columbia and Alberta, where Chinese migrants mined for gold; the black Loyalists in Preston and their waves of relocation by the British; maroons from Jamaica deported to Nova Scotia, granted less land in surveys for sharecropping than whites; the *Komagata Maru,* which brought British subjects from Punjab, British India, to Canada, and who were refused entry by the racist Canadian exclusion laws; the waves and waves of nonarrival and the uncertainty that can never reassuringly assert "you are Here" to confirm your place in the universe: this "unbearable archaeology" (Brand 1997, 73) of the geologic codes of dispossession time-travel to arrive in the racist impulse of the white cop who stops three friends in a snowstorm on the way to Buxton. These material histories sediment and arrive in the now as a continued challenge to presence in the context of erasure. They arrive as a geophysics of sense.

In *Listening to Images,* Campt develops an idea of "tense" as an affectual force of politics, enacting a movement toward a different theoretical possibility through the destabilization of the mode of encounter, listening rather than seeing the quiet soundings, blurring the authority of the visual code. She reorganizes the aesthetic sense of engagement away from the dominant reading of images as visual to attenuate both attention and a mode of reading resistance through tense (of the poise and noise of black bodies). Campt's (2017, 16) work on photography's quiet registers of meaning identifies an undercurrent in which we might read "possibilities obliquely . . . the tiny, often miniscule chinks and crevices of what appears to be the inescapable web of capture" in the "terms and tenses of grammar," undercurrents that travel through more surface-led summations. She argues that the future can be conceived in terms of acts and political movements, but "I believe we must not only look but also listen for it in other, less likely places . . . in some of the least celebrated, often most disposable archives" (16). That is, decentering Eurocentric logics is not just a theoretical exercise of decolonization but a realignment of sense through affective infrastructures, an affective mattering in the discourse of materiality and its worlds. Campt says,

> Futurity is, for me, not a question of "hope"—though it is certainly inescapably intertwines with the idea of aspiration. To me it is crucial to think about futurity through a notion of "tense." What is the "tense" of a black feminist future? It is a tense of anteriority, a tense relationship to an idea of possibility that is neither innocent nor naïve. Nor is it necessarily heroic or intentional. It is often humble and strategic, subtle and discriminating. It is devious and exacting. It's not always loud and demanding. It is frequently quiet and opportunistic, dogged and disruptive. (17)

Campt's understanding of new arrangements of sense that are counterintuitive to the directional flow of readings that take place within the intellectual framework of Western liberalism enacts an axiological redirection of sense into new theoretical possibilities (affectual possibilities within the tight spaces of the quotidian rather than on their outsides). Reiterating Wynter's call to take the senses as theoreticians, this unsettles sense and settles it into new formations that have a political charge precisely because they have a subterranean force that travels underneath and through colonial technologies of space and time. The printmaker's gentle craft is to not subject the woman out the women to the gravitational field, to give her, or rather let her claim, another geophysics of being that does not subject her to an "inevitable" geo-logics of her designated material and symbolic position (a position that she has already claimed for herself in her leap). White Geology offers a geophysics of anti-Blackness, but the black woman held in countergravity expands the dimensions of geologic force through a different tense of possibility and relation to the earth. Rather than being framed in the "vexed genealogy of freedom" that forged the liberal imagination through "entanglements of bondage and liberty" (Hartman 1997, 115), she is partaking of a different gravitational opening, in Césaire's ([1972] 2000, 42) words, "made to the measure of the world."

In the lexicon of geology that takes possession of people and places, delimiting the organization of existence, the refusal of such captivity makes a commons in the measure and pitch of the world, not the exclusive universality of the humanist subject. I think of all the forced stoniness[2] that I have read in this past year through the literatures of slavery and its afterlives, the brittle broken rocks and bones forced together in mines, in the cut of cane on the plantation, the stoniness of bodies held against the imagination of a black life as an empty sign of property that positioned them as a receptacle for white desire and violence (per Hartman), the endurance of a stony patience that doesn't forget love. Rather, this rock poetry finds that love is in the oceanic of the earth. As Brand (1997, 46) imagines slaves on factory ships, whose crank of the neck and

2. Wynter (n.d., 128) describes how, in colonizers' descriptions of slave crucifixion, slaves appeared to them as little affected by their sadistic torture, "behaving all the time with a degree of hardened insolence, and brutal insensibility," suggesting an inability on the colonizers' part to perceive the sensibility of black pain or to understand the courage marshaled against it.

tip of the boat reveal for a moment the horizon, "they moving toward their own bone . . . 'so thank god for the ocean and the sky
all implicated, all unconcerned,' they must have said, 'or there'd be
nothing to love.'" Lilting, in the shit of the hold and the tip of the
waves, "stripped in their life, naked as seaweed, they would have
sat and sunk but no, the sky was a doorway, a famine and a jacket."
A refusal to be delimited is found in the matter of the world and a
home in its maroonage; "they wander as if they have no century,
as if they can bound time . . . compasses whose directions tilt, skid
off known maps" (46).

Refusal might be understood in terms of the friendship of the
"No" that Maurice Blanchot ([1971] 1997, 111–12) locates in the resistance to torture or oppression (perhaps influenced by his own
experience in front of a firing squad)—a refusal that affirms the
break or the rupture from an unacceptable logic and reason:

> What we refuse is not without value or importance. This is precise-
> ly why refusal is necessary. There is a kind of reason that we will
> no longer accept, there is an appearance of wisdom that horrifies
> us, there is an offer of agreement and compromise that we will not
> hear. A rupture has occurred. We have been to this frankness that
> does not tolerate complicity any longer. When we refuse, we refuse
> with a movement free from contempt and exaltation, one that is as
> far as possible anonymous, for the power of refusal is accomplished
> neither by us nor in our name, but from a very poor beginning that
> belongs first of all to those who cannot speak . . . refusal is never easy,
> that we must learn how to refuse and to maintain intact this power of
> refusal, by the rigor of thinking and modesty of expression that each
> one of our affirmations must evidence from now on.

Tilting the axis of engagement within a geological optic and intimacy, the inhuman can be claimed as a different kind of resource
than in its propertied colonial form—a gravitational force so ex-
travagant, it defies gravity.

Forging a new language of geology must provide a lexicon with
which to take apart the Anthropocene, a poetry to refashion a new
epoch, a new geology that attends to the racialization of matter
(see Silva 2017). Turning to critical black aesthetics is not an at-

tempt to reformulate the Anthropocene into a different scene through black ontologies, ontologies without territories, but to locate more precisely how the praxis of that aesthetic, forged as it was within the context of inhuman intimacies that are inherently antiblack (constituted by the material geographies of colonialism, slavery, and diaspora), locates an insurgent geology. The origins of the Anthropocene continue to erasure and dissimulate violent histories of encounter, dispossession, and death in the geographical imagination. This geologic prehistory has everything to do with the Anthropocene as a condition of the present; it is the material history that constitutes the present in all its geotraumas and thus should be embraced, reworked, and reconstituted in terms of agency *for* the present, *for the end of this world* and the possibility of others, because the world is already turning to face the storm, writing its weather for the geology next time. We are all, after all, involved in geology, from the cosmic mineralogical constitution of our bodies to the practices and aesthetics that fuel our consumption and ongoing extraction. Our desire is constituted in the underground, shaped in the mine and the dark seams of forgotten formations that one day we will become, that we are already becoming. But our relation to the underground is different.

Inside the language of inhuman proximities, the ghosts of geology rise, naming storms, tornados, leaves, and rivers as experience. Césaire (quoted in Brand 2001, 58) writes,

> I should discover once again the secret of great
> Communication and great combustions ...
>
> I have words vast enough to
> contain you and you, earth, tense drunken earth ...

Writing a Geology for the Storm Next Time

My own effort is to try to bear witness to something that will
have to be there when the storm is over, to help us get through
the next storm. Storms are always coming.

—JAMES BALDWIN, quoted in Ed Pavlic, *"Who Can Afford to
Improvise?": James Baldwin and Black Music, the Lyric and the Listeners*

To travel without a map, to travel without a way. They did,
long ago. That misdirection became the way. After the Door
of No Return, a map was only a set of impossibilities, a set of
changing locations.

—DIONNE BRAND, *A Map to the Door of No Return: Notes to
Belonging*

A Billion Black Anthropocenes is a mediation on the politics
and poetics of abjection that underpin the becoming of the
Anthropocene as a material and durational fact in bodies and
environments: a subtended geology that differentiates and is differentiating in relations of power. Geologists may say, what has
this got to do with geology, to which may be replied, everything!
The Anthropocene was conceived as a political geology, and
that is its practice, and besides, historically, when was geology
anything but political in its narratives about the world, origins,
and the weaponization of extraction as a motivation and mode
of dispossession? Deep-time and near-time geologic questions
are entangled with hard political questions about decolonizing

and the possibility of futures. Noticing the meshwork of anti-Blackness and colonial structures of the Anthropocene, which constitute the distinct underbelly to its origin stories, gives visibility to the material and bodily work that coercively carries the Anthropocene into being and challenges the narrative accounts of agency there within. That is, the survival of these *geologic surrogates* disrupts, shows up, and contests the easy accounts of colonial universalism and its reproduction of power geometries in geological life. I want to alter how we think and imagine geological relations in nonextractive modes, to think about encountering the coming storm in ways that do not facilitate its permeant renewal. Regardless of the political weather that conditions the terminology around environmental rupture, there is no getting away from the radical presencing of geology in our lives, as energy, sensibility, storm, rift, and a growing awareness of what that energy costs across corporeal and planetary bodies (an awareness that has had its "quieted" witnesses since 1492). When the storm is over, there will be another. The storms are always coming, with faster and greater intensity. From a very literal point of view, these storms might very well be the loudest and most insistent political message and material instantiation of the Anthropocene today. If today's storm is a prelude to another, what, in Baldwin's words, would help us get through the storm next time?

A tentative movement toward the decolonialization of the Anthropocene might be made through geo-Poethics. Geo-Poethics takes up Silva's use of the term Poethics to denote a black feminist praxis that might actively announce a whole way of knowing, doing, existing, as an ethical mandate. Silva (2014) says, "What is Black Poethic Intention? Is it an ethics, which instead of the betterment of the World as we know it aims at its end?" Such an Anthropocene geo-Poethics would turn against Man and the homogenizing impulse of humanist tropes into and another world of matter that puts race as central to the geosocial and geo-Poethical formations of the Anthropocene. This geo-

Poethical tension might propel us toward the idea of a billion Black Anthropocenes as an unsettling in Anthropocenic thought. I have argued that the Anthropocene exhibits a *colonial geology,* a geology in which spikes are named and conceived, which in turn generates a specifically racialized territorialization of the earth. In light of this colonialism and how geomorphic moments are marked in the flesh of targeted communities, there is a need both to rethink the empirics of this social geology—that is, to pay attention to the material composition of these geologic moments—and epistemically not to reproduce those arrangements of power in the telling. Currently we have a White Anthropocene that transforms the epistemic traditions of the particular into a general expression without "refashioning at a collective level" the terms of humanity (Silva 2015, 99).

How is it possible to dislodge the language of geology so that such dispossessing movements cannot be so easily made? This is a question of redress that frames the Anthropocene in the alchemy of race and geology as a calculus of extraction. If the Anthropocene prompts a recognition of the change in quality of the subjective force of geology, it must do so at a material level in the ways that geologic relations structure, sustain, condition, and constrain agency. And it must do so at a symbolic level, to challenge the ways in which geologic classification organizes psychic lives and modes of nonbeing. That is to think about how "geopower" (Yusoff 2018) is a product of subjugating relations as well as geopolitical consideration and capitalization rather than to reinforce and reiterate the "naturalization" of colonial dispossession of land and minerals. This historic analysis extends concern for the contemporary subjects caught in dehumanizing geologic relations that deform the earth in various ways (which is recognized in the Anthropocene) and that deform subjects (which is not explicitly recognized). Rarely are these twinned structural deformations thought together as an epistemic praxis that finds its resolution in inhuman relation. Who is protected by such a division in these inhuman structures? How does geologic nomenclature space the distance between these two conjoined operations? If the imagination of planetary peril coerces an ideal of "we," it only does so when the entrappings of late liberalism become threatened. This "we" negates all responsibility for how the wealth of that geology was built off the subtending strata of indigenous genocide and erasure, slavery and carceral labor, and evades what that accumulation of wealth still makes possible in the present—lest "we" forget that the economies of geology still largely regulate geopolitics and modes of naturalizing, formalizing, and operationalizing dispossession and ongoing settler colonialism.

What would a geology look like that refused its role as formulated by the adage that Charles Lyell famously coined—"the key to the past lies in the present"—and moved, instead, with the anticipatory geologic formations of the Anthropocene, a formulation that explicitly recognizes that the key to the future lies in the present and that the present is not just future oriented but that the future is already inscripted in the present, already bounding with the material recombinations of the bad material formulations of the past secreted into future possibilities? Writing a geology for the storm next time would move away from the immediate political gratification of naming a Golden Spike or being author of a new origin story into the historical record of a geology that is at once destabilizing of the historicity that it carries and cognizant of the bloody catalog that it has marked. A set of questions emerges from this derangement of geology:

1. How does the formation of the Anthropocene as a political geology reformulate and reimagine material relations that have hitherto been organized by anti-Blackness?

2. What displacements of violence go into this maneuver to organize around an "innocent" geologic subjectivity in the pursuit of a future environmental citizenship? What strategies of individuation and communing are involved in the geologizing of the social?

3. Who is vulnerable to injury by the idea of the Anthropocene, epistemologically and materially, in the erasure of differentiated

effects and sharing of the surplus? In parallel, what becomes invulnerable to scrutiny?

4. How do these propositions of geologic life in the Anthropocene
   organize and manage a set of relations in a regulatory framing of
   propertied and properties? What are the normative presupposi-
   tions of geology as a way of operating and extending settler colonialism through the nomenclature of materiality and the praxis of
   extractions?

5. Since geology is a hinge that joins indigenous genocide, slavery,
   and settler colonialism through an indifferent structure of extraction, indifferent to the specifies of people and places, how
   does the refusal of responsibility in the mapping of pasts and futures of geology leave the present unchecked?

A Billion Black Anthropocenes proposes a new graphia of geology that unearths the racial secretions in its historic and future
praxis. Rather than seeing Blackness as biopolitical, we might
also see it as a geopolitical act in the division of flesh and earth
though the grammar of the inhuman. What I propose is that the
Anthropocene produces a geophysics of anti-Blackness enacted
through sets of material and psychic relations in the designation
of property and properties. The championing of the collective in
geology under the guise of universality or humanity is actually a
deformation of the differentiation of subjective relations made in
and through geology. This is how the codification of geology (as
land, mineral, metal, gold, commodity, value, resource) becomes
the historical basis of theft, actioning a field of dispossession in
which the language of containment is used to materially organize extraction, where violence is covered in the guise of liber-
ating surplus wealth from people and the earth. *A Billion Black
Anthropocenes* goes in search of a grammar of geology for the
storm next time. It proposes that the event of geology become
truly marked by the colonial marks that have instigated its passage across the "measure of the world" (Césaire [1972] 2000, 73).
It embraces its intimacies with the inhuman. It asserts an insurgent geology for the end of the world, for the possibility of other

worlds not marked by anti-Blackness, where the inhuman is a relation, no longer an appendage of fungibility. It is a refusal of the white overburden of geology that has secreted its excess into every pore of the earth. No geology is neutral.

The problem was gravity and the answer was gravity. (Brand 2014, 157)

Acknowledgments

This work started out as a response to a call from Angela Last, who organized a workshop on "Decolonizing the Anthropocene" in 2015. The ideas and text have metamorphosed many times since, in response to attendance at too many Anthropocene events, where the absence of discussions of race allowed the smooth flow of patriarchal reason to make its earth anew. The citation practice I have followed reflects these absences. My aim in this book was to open a space for these critical discussions about race and geology, because women, especially women of color, if citation practices are to be believed, do not write theories of the earth, and if the same citation practices are to be adhered to, they don't write much of anything, expect their own erasure! Specifically, I am grateful for invitations from Astrida Neimanis and Jennifer Mae Hamilton (Sydney University, "Hacking the Anthropocene: Feminist, Queer and Anticolonial Propositions," April 2016), Rory Rowan (University of Zurich, "The Anthropocene between Earth and Social Sciences," November 2016), Jody Dean (Fisher Center for the Study of Women and Men, Hobart and William Smith Colleges, "Gender, Climate, and the Anthropocene," February 2016), the New Materialism Conference (Paris UNESCO, "Environmental Humanities and New Materialisms: The Ethics of Decolonizing Nature and Culture," June 2017), Andrew Baldwin (Durham University, December 2017), and the London Group of Historical Geographers (Institute for Historical Research, November 2017). I am especially grateful for helpful comments on and critical responses to this work as I learned my way through the literatures of black studies and geology. A special shout-out to Stephanie Springgay and Sarah E. Truman for the sprint to issue me with my "queer trails" badge in Paris. I am grateful to the Schomburg Center for Research in Black Culture, where I read Sylvia Wynter's extraordinary "Black Metamorphosis" and James Baldwin's essays, and to the archives of the Smithsonian National Museum of Natural History and the incredible National Museum of African American History and Culture. The team at University of Minnesota Press have been enthusiastic throughout this process, and especial thanks are due to Dani Kasprzak, Jason Weidman, and Anne Carter. The text was finally written up during a fellowship at the Institute of Advanced Studies, Durham University. Without that concentrated time and the fine fellowship encountered there, this work would never have been made into this (small) book. For friendship and food during the storms, thanks are due to Lisa, Andrew, Lorcan and Torin, Amanda and Pete, Robyn, and, in Durham, the "Fellows," Divya Tolia-Kelly, Siobhán McGrath, Elizabeth Johnson, and Andrew Baldwin. Thinking with shapes where the writing ends up. For keeping the fires burning and the humor sharp in the End of the World "comms," I thank Jennifer Gabrys, Tim Pearn, Myra Hird, Nigel Clark, Angela Last, and Stephanie Wakefield. In its most joyous releases and subterranean modes, thought is a conversation made on the shuttle back and forth. I have had the pleasure of having longtime interlocutors about the inhuman in Nigel Clark and Myra Hird, and the deep-time provocations of Mary Thomas have changed that thinking in all its orientations.

Bibliography

Baldwin, James, and Margaret Mead. 1971. *Rap on Race*. New York: Bantam Double Day Dell.

Bebbington, Anthony J., and Jeffrey T. Bury. 2013. "Institutional Challenges for Mining and Sustainability in Peru." *PNAS* 106, no. 41: 17296–301.

Blackman, Douglas. 2008. *Slavery by Another Name*. New York: Anchor Books.

Blanchot, Maurice. (1971) 1997. *Friendship*. Stanford, Calif.: Stanford University Press.

Bogues, Antony, ed. 2006. *After Man, towards the Human: Critical Essays on Sylvia Wynter*. Kingston, U.K.: Ian Randle.

Brand, Dionne. 1996. *In Another Place, Not Here*. Toronto: Vintage Canada.

Brand, Dionne. 1997. *Land to Light On*. Toronto, Ont.: McClelland and Stewart.

Brand, Dionne. 1999. *At the Full and Change of the Moon*. New York: Grove Press.

Brand, Dionne. 2001. *A Map to the Door of No Return: Notes to Belonging*. Vancouver, B.C.: Random House.

Brand, Dionne. 2014. *Love Enough*. Vancouver, B.C.: Random House.

Brand, Dionne. 2017a. "An *Ars Poetica* from the Blue Clerk." *The Black Scholar* 47, no. 1: 58–77.

Brand, Dionne. 2017b. "Writing against Tyranny and toward Liberation." Barnard Center for Research on Women. https://www.youtube.com/watch?v=eCbktO7pOuY.

Broeck, Sabine, and Carsten Junker, eds. 2014. *Postcoloniality–Decoloniality–Black Critique: Joints and Fissures*. Frankfurt, Germany: Campus.

Buck-Morss, Susan. 2000. "Hegel and Haiti." *Critical Inquiry* 26, no. 4: 821–65.

Butler, Judith. 2015. *Senses of the Subject*. New York: Fordham University Press.

Campt, Tina. 2017. *Listening to Images*. Durham, N.C.: Duke University Press.

Césaire, Aimé. (1956) 1969. *Return to My Native Land*. New York: Archipelago Books.

Césaire, Aimé. (1972) 2000. *Discourse on Colonialism*. New York: Monthly Review Press.

Crutzen, Paul. 2002. "Geology of Mankind—the Anthropocene." *Nature* 415: 23.

Crutzen, Paul, and Christian Schwäger. 2011. "Living in the Anthropocene: Towards a new Global Ethos." http://e360.yale.edu /features/living_in_the_anthropocene_toward_a_new_global_ethos.

Davies, Carole B. 2015. "From Masquerade to *Maskarade*: Caribbean Cultural Resistance and Rehumanizing Project." In *Sylvia Wynter: On Being Human as Praxis,* edited by Katherine McKittrick, 203–25. Durham, N.C.: Duke University Press.

DeLoughrey, Elizabeth. 2013. "The Myth of Isolates: Ecosystem Ecologies in the Nuclear Pacific." *Cultural Geographies* 20: 167–84.

Dhairyam, Sagri. 2017. "'Artifacts for Survival': Remapping the Contours of Poetry with Audre Lorde." *Feminist Studies* 18, no. 2: 229–56.

Du Bois, W. E. B. 1920. *Darkwater: Voices from within the Veil*. New York: Harcourt, Brace.

Fanon, Franz. 1963. *The Wretched of the Earth*. New York: Grove Press.

Glissant, Édouard. 1997. *Poetics of Relation*. Ann Arbor: University Press of Michigan.

Gumbs, Alexis P. 2017. "Coal: Black Matter Oracle." *The Black Scholar* 47, no. 3: 3–7.

Hall, Catherine. 2014. "Gendering Property, Racing Capital." *History Workshop Journal* 78: 22–38.

Hartman, Saidiya. 1997. *Scenes of Subjection: Terror, Slavery, and Self-Making in Nineteenth-Century America*. Oxford: Oxford University Press.

Hartman, Saidiya. 2002. "The Time of Slavery." *South Atlantic Quarterly* 101, no. 4: 757–77.

Hartman, Saidiya. 2007. *Lose Your Mother: A Journey along the Atlantic Slave Route*. New York: Farrar, Straus, and Giroux.

Hartman, Saidiya, and Frank Wilderson. 2003. "The Position of the Unthought." *Qui Parle* 13, no. 2: 183–201.

James, C. L. R. (1938) 1989. *Black Jacobins: Toussaint L'Ouverture and the San Domingo Revolution*. New York: Random House.

King, Tiffany L. 2016. "The Labor of (Re)reading Plantation Landscapes Fungibile(ly)." *Antipode* 48, no. 2: 1022–1039.

Kuletz, Valerie. 1998. *The Tainted Desert: Environmental Ruin in the American West*. New York: Routledge.

Last, Angela. 2015. "Fruit of the Cyclone: Undoing Geopolitics through Geopoetics." *Geoforum* 64: 56–64.

Last, Angela. 2017. "We Are the World? Anthropocene Cultural Production between Geopoetics and Geopolitics." *Theory, Culture, and Society* 34: 147–68.

Laubscher, Laetitia. 2017. "Between the Devil and the Deep Blue: Marshall Islanders Face Nuclear Fallout and Rising Seas." *Vice,* March 7. https:// www.vice.com/en_nz/article/pgwg5y/between-the-devil-and-the -deep-blue-marshall-islanders-face-nuclear-fallout-and-rising-seas.

LeMenager, Stephanie. 2014. *Living Oil: Petroleum Culture in the American Century.* Oxford: Oxford University Press.

Lewis, Simon, and Mark Maslin. 2015. "Defining the Anthropocene." *Nature* 519: 171–180.

Lorde, Audre. 1984. "Revolutionary Hope: A Conversation between James Baldwin and Audre Lorde." December 1984. Box 5, folder 16, James Baldwin Archive, Schomburg Center.

Lorde, Audre. 1996. *Coal.* London: W. W. Norton.

Lyell, Charles. 1845. *Travels in North America.* London: John Murray.

Lyell, Charles. 1849. *A Second Visit to the United States of North America.* London: John Murray.

Malm, Andreas. 2015. *Fossil Capitalism.* London: Verso.

Martin, Edwin J., and Richard H. Rowland. 1982. *Castle Series, 1951.* Defense Nuclear Agency Report DNA 6035F. April 1. http://worf.eh .doe.gov/data/ihp1c/0858_a.pdf.

Marx, Karl. (1867) 1961. *Capital.* Vol. 1. Moscow: Progress.

McKittrick, Katherine. 2011. "On Plantations, Prisons, and a Black Sense of Place." *Social and Cultural Geography* 12, no. 8: 947–63.

Mintz, Sidney. 1985. *Sweetness and Power: The Place of Sugar in Modern History.* New York: Viking.

Mbembe, Achille. 2017. *A Critique of Black Reason.* Durham, N.C.: Duke University Press.

Morrison, Toni. 1992. *Playing in the Dark: Whiteness and the Literary Imagination.* New York: Vintage.

Moten, Fred. 2003. *In the Break: The Aesthetics of the Black Radical Tradition.* Minneapolis: University of Minnesota Press.

Moten, Fred. 2016. *A Poetics of the Undercommons.* N.p.: Sputnik and Fizzle.

Moten, Fred, and S. Harney. 2013. *The Undercommons: Fugitive Planning and Black Study.* Minor Compositions. New York: Autonomedia.

Povinelli, Elizabeth A. 2016. *Geonotologies: A Requiem to Late Liberalism.* Durham, N.C.: Duke University Press.

Robbins, Nicholas. 2011. *Mercury, Mining, and Empire: The Human and Ecological Cost of Silver Mining in the Andes.* Bloomington: Indiana University Press.

Sexton, Jared. 2010. "People-of-Color-Blindness." *Social Text* 28, no. 2: 31–55.

Sharpe, Christina. 2009. *Monstrous Intimacies: Making Post-Slavery Subjects*. Durham, N.C.: Duke University Press.

Sharpe, Christina. 2016a. *In the Wake: On Blackness and Being*. Durham, N.C.: Duke University Press.

Sharpe, Christina. 2016b. "Lose Your Kin." *New Inquiry,* November 16. https://thenewinquiry.com/lose-your-kin/.

Silva, Denise F. 2007. *Toward a Global Idea of Race*. Minneapolis: University of Minnesota Press.

Silva, Denise F. 2014. "Toward a Black Feminist Poethics." *The Black Scholar* 44, no. 2: 81–97.

Silva, Denise F. 2015. "Before Man: Sylvia Wynter's Rewriting of the Modern Episteme." In *Sylvia Wynter: On Being Human as Praxis,* edited by Katherine McKittrick, 90–105. Durham, N.C.: Duke University Press.

Silva, Denise F. 2017. "–1 (life) ÷ 0 (blackness) = $\infty - \infty$ or ∞ / ∞: On Matter beyond the Equation of Value." *E-Flux* 79. https://www.e-flux.com/journal/79/94686/1-life-0-blackness-or-on-matter-beyond-the-equation-of-value/.

Spillers, Hortense J. 2003. *Black, White and in Colour*. Chicago: University of Chicago Press.

Synder, Terri L. 2015. *The Power to Die: Slavery and Suicide in British North America*. Chicago: University of Chicago Press.

Taussig, Michael. 1986. *Shamanism, Colonialism, and the Wild Man: A Study in Terror and Healing*. Chicago: University of Chicago Press.

Tuck, Eve, and K. Wayne Yang. 2012. "Decolonization Is Not a Metaphor." *Decolonization: Indigeneity, Education, and Society* 1, no. 1: 1–40.

Waters, Colin N., Jan Zalasiewicz, Colin Summerhayes, Anthony D. Barnosky, Clément Poirier, Agnieszka Gałuszka, Alejandro Cearreta et al. 2016. "The Anthropocene Is Functionally and Stratigraphically Distinct from the Holocene." *Science* 351, no. 6269. https://doi.org/10.1126/science.aad2622.

Weheliye, Alexander. 2002. "Freenin' Posthuman Voices in Contemporary Black Popular Music." *Social Text* 20, no. 2: 20–47.

Weheliye, Alexander. 2014. *Habeas Viscus: Racializing Assemblages, Biopolitics, and Black Theories of the Human*. Durham, N.C.: Duke University Press.

Wilderston, Frank, III. 2008. *Incognegro*. Durham, N.C.: Duke University Press.

Wright, Michelle. 2015. *Physics of Blackness: Beyond the Middle Passage Epistemology*. Minneapolis: University of Minnesota Press.

Wynter, Sylvia. 2015. "Unparalleled Catastrophe for Our Species? Or, to Give Humanness a Different Future: Conversations." In *Sylvia Wynter: On Being Human as Praxis,* edited by Katherine McKittrick, 9–89. Durham, N.C.: Duke University Press.

Wynter, Sylvia. N.d. "Black Metamorphosis: New Natives in a New World." Institute of the Black World Records, MG 502, Box 1. Schomburg Center for Research in Black Culture.

Yusoff, Kathryn. 2013. "Geologic Life: Prehistory, Climate, Futures in the Anthropocene." *Environment and Planning D: Society and Space* 31, no. 5: 779–795.

Yusoff, Kathryn. 2015. "Queer Coal: Genealogies in/of the Blood, SI on Anthropocene." *PhiloSOPHIA: Journal of Continental Feminism* 5, no. 2: 203–230.

Yusoff, Kathryn. 2016. "Anthropogenesis: Origins and Endings in the Anthropocene." *Theory, Culture, and Society* 33, no. 2: 3–28.

Yusoff, Kathryn. 2017a. "Epochal Aesthetics." *E-Flux.* http://www.e-flux .com/architecture/accumulation/121847/epochal-aesthetics-affectual -infrastructures-of-the-anthropocene/.

Yusoff, Kathryn. 2017b. "Politics of the Anthropocene: Formation of the Commons as a Geologic Process." *Antipode: A Radical Journal of Geography* 50, no. 1: 255–76.

Yusoff, Kathryn. 2018. "The Anthropocene and Geographies of Geopower." In *Geographies of Power,* edited by M. Coleman and J. Agnew, 203–16. London: Edward Elgar.

Yusoff, Kathryn, and Mary Thomas. 2018. "Anthropocene." In *Edinburgh Companion to Animal Studies,* edited by L. Turner, U. Undine Sellbach, and R. Broglio, 52–64. Edinburgh: Edinburgh University Press.

Zalasiewicz, Jan, Colin N. Waters, Mark Williams et al. 2015. "When Did the Anthropocene Begin? A Mid-Twentieth Century Boundary Level is Stratigraphically Optimal." *Quaternary International* 383, no. 5: 196–203.

Kathryn Yusoff is professor of inhuman geography at Queen Mary University of London.